W9-AXI-877

ASQC
LIBRARY

TS
155
.I 7313  1991
C.2

# IE FOR THE SHOP FLOOR
## Productivity Through Motion Study

# IE FOR THE SHOP FLOOR

Volume 1: Productivity Through Process Analysis
*Junichi Ishiwata*

Volume 2: Productivity Through Motion Study
*Kenichirō Katō*

# IE FOR THE SHOP FLOOR

## Productivity Through Motion Study

Kenichirō Katō

Foreword by
Jim Guzzo
Westinghouse Productivity
and Quality Center

Publisher's Message by
Norman Bodek
President, Productivity, Inc.

**Productivity Press, Inc.**
Cambridge, Massachusetts    Norwalk, Connecticut

Originally published as *Gemba no IE (II): dōsa bunseki (Worksite IE (II): Motion Study)*, Volume 10 in the *Gemba QC dokuhon (New worksite QC primer)* series compiled by the QC Circle magazine editorial group and published by JUSE Press, Ltd., 1983, 1988. Copyright © 1983 Kenichirō Katō.

English translation copyright © 1991 Productivity Press, Inc.
Translated by Bruce Talbot.

All rights reserved. No part of this book may be reproduced or utilized in any form or by any means, electronic or mechanical, including photocopying, recording, or by any information storage and retrieval system, without permission in writing from the publisher. Additional copies of this book are available from the publisher. Address all inquiries to:

Productivity Press
P.O. Box 3007
Cambridge, Massachusetts 02140
United States of America
Telephone: (617) 497-5146
Telefax: (617) 868-3524

Cover design by David B. Lennon and Susan Q. Cobb
Printed and bound by BookCrafters
Printed in the United States of America
Printed on acid-free paper

**Library of Congress Cataloging-in-Publication Data**

Ishiwata, Junichi.
   [Genba no IE. English]
   IE for the shop floor / cJunichi Ishiwata ; [translated by Bruce Talbot].
   2 v. ; cm.
   Translation of: Genba no IE.
   Vol. 2 written by Katō Ken'ichirō
   Contents: 1. Productivity through process analysis — 2. Productivity through motion study.
   ISBN 0-915299-82-8 (v. 1).
   ISBN 1-56327-000-5 (v. 2).
   1. Factory management. 2. Production control. 3. Quality circles.
I. Katō, Ken'ichirō, 1947- . II. Title.
TS155.I7313   1991                                                                91-2193
670.4--dc20                                                                            CIP

91 92 93 10 9 8 7 6 5 4 3 2 1

# Contents

# Publisher's Message

It is a pleasure to present *Productivity Through Motion Study*, the second volume of a four-part set, *IE for the Shop Floor*.

Since their "discovery" by Frederick Taylor, the Gilbreths, and other early pioneers, industrial engineering methods in manufacturing plants have improved productivity tremendously over the years. Ford Motor was one of the early experimenters. Using IE methods in the first part of this century, the Ford production system was able to double the output of automobiles — and double the wages of the workers.

The focal point of industrial engineering is the improvement of productivity. Using IE and quality improvement methodologies, Western companies have made enormous strides in the past. Traditionally, these tools were placed in the hands of specialists. Professional engineers and managers were often the exclusive decision makers in these issues, despite the inherent expertise of the shop floor people who did the job every day and best knew the situation. Management rarely asked these workers for their improvement ideas or trained them in ways to analyze the situation.

Today we know there has to be a different approach to the improvement of quality and productivity. Over the last 10 to 12 years, we have seen the difference in results of companies in which only specialists can make a change, and those in which every individual, from the CEO to the newest hourly worker, is committed to continuous improvement. The Japanese have shown us that we can't afford not to involve every member of the company in this drive. *Everyone* in the company must be aware that he or she can make a difference in the vitality of the company — and must be educated, given the tools, and empowered to make that difference.

Industrial engineering is a complex science that has developed in great depth and in a number of diverse yet related directions. Yet from this detailed knowledge, a set of simple and effective techniques can be extracted and applied directly to improve work in manufacturing plants.

The unique value of this set of books is its accessible approach to the material. They were not written for engineers in offices far removed from the production line, but rather for the training of supervisors and workers right where the action is — on the shop floor.

With the new audience for these methods comes a new frame of reference about how they can be used. These books are not about work analysis methods as a management control tool. This is industrial engineering for the workers themselves to use. It is participative, employee-involved IE.

The approach described in these books is rooted in an understanding of the value of *kaizen,* or continuous improvement. To successfully compete on quality, cost, and delivery, large-scale innovation is simply not enough. The world's leading manufacturing companies are ahead today because their employees — from the executive suite to the drafting room to the shop floor — are constantly fine-tuning their processes and looking for even small ways to improve the work.

You are probably familiar with many of the tools of kaizen — improvement teams have been using the 7 QC Tools, the 7 New Tools, and related methods for years. With this set, four basic IE methods join the tool kit to increase the range of improvement possibilities.

*Productivity Through Motion Study* is in a sense a more refined level of the process analysis approach described in the first volume of the set. Rather than following the various steps a product or an operator goes through during an entire process, motion study analyzes the movements of a worker in the course of an individual operation or series of operations. Though on different scales, the basic aims of the two methods are similar — to eliminate unnecessary steps — with an additional emphasis on redesigning awkward movements to avoid fatigue, prevent mistakes, and speed the flow of work.

The book describes several of the key methods used for visualizing a worker's movements for motion study. Some of these methods have become the basis for a number of highly refined work analysis systems used by engineers. *Productivity Through Motion Study*, however, focuses on a simple method called *therblig analysis* to describe operations in terms of 18 basic motions. All motions are not equal; some are less necessary or desirable than others. One of the points of therblig analysis is to get rid of as many non-value-adding motions as possible.

In addition to a thorough introduction to how to use therblig analysis, the *Productivity Through Motion Study* elaborates on 11 "checkpoints" for motion economy — important tips to consider when evaluating an individual's movements during work. The final chapter presents two full-length case studies showing the application of these methods to improve actual factory situations.

We hope that these powerful techniques become part of your company's competitive advantage in the hands of your supervisors and team leaders.

I would like to express my thanks to the author, Kenichirō Katō, for his clear discussion of motion study, to Zenichirō Kurita, president of JUSE Press, and to Katsuharu Arai, director of the editorial department of JUSE Press, for permitting us to translate these valuable books. I am also grateful to Akira Kashima of the Japan Foreign-Rights Centre for facilitating the publishing arrangements. Thanks especially to Jim Guzzo, senior consultant at Westinghouse Productivity and Quality Center and a leading expert in manufacturing process improvement, for contributing an excellent foreword to the book. Steven Ott, vice president and general manager of Productivity Press, has my appreciation for producing these English editions.

A special thanks to the many people who helped produce these books: to Bruce Talbot, for his fine translation; to Karen Jones for editorial development of the text and figures; to Mugi Hanao for special editorial assistance with translation questions; to Marie Cantlon and Dorothy Lohmann for managing the manuscript editing, with the assistance of Christine Carvajal (copyediting), Leslie Macmillan and James Rolwing (word processing), Aurelia Navarro (proofreading), and Jennifer Cross (indexing); to Kathlin Sweeney for managing the production of the book; to David Lennon for designing the covers; and to Gayle Joyce, Susan Cobb, Jane Donovan, Caroline Kutil, Gary Ragaglia, Michele Saar, and Karla Tolbert for typesetting and the professional preparation of the illustrations.

Norman Bodek
President
Productivity, Inc.

# Foreword

The modern approach to process improvement, a critical aspect of total quality in high-volume manufacturing, begins with an analysis of cycle time. Overall cycle time has three main components: setup time, run time, and time involving queues or delays. These are most effectively addressed in the reverse of the order given. After using methods such as process analysis to reduce non-value-adding delays, the operating time can be reduced, and finally the obstacle of long setup times can be made a nonissue through quick changeover techniques.

These improvements to cycle time are major adjustments that should be well under way before a company ever turns to motion study, the subject of this book. Motion study is a method for fine-tuning the major adjustments. As with any mechanism for fine adjustments, its effectiveness depends on first getting to a point where a focused approach will do some good. Doing motion study before attacking process delays would be like setting out to carve Mount Rushmore with dental tools.

Appropriate use of motion study techniques does improve the efficiency and productivity of individual workers. Even more than that, however, it is a method that employees themselves can use to improve the quality of their lives at work and after work. Motion study is, above all, about avoiding fatigue in order to perform the work correctly, safely, and with energy to bring home to one's personal life.

*Productivity Through Motion Study* represents a progressive tool for all employees in companies where high-volume repetitive manufacturing is a fundamental way of doing business. The individual techniques introduced here are not new; therbligs were first developed and used in the 1920s. The book's progressiveness lies in its emphasis on equipping *the employees themselves* with these techniques to improve the quality of life at work while effecting corporate improvement.

The improvement of quality and profitability absolutely requires strategic human resource development. As we move through the continuous improvement process in total quality, doing the right things right the first time, it is imperative that we continue to substantially raise the skill levels of all employees. We must make it a priority to equip workers with the proper techniques and tools that allow them to effectively change the workplace and enhance the quality of life.

Motion study, as a final step in the process of improving a high-volume manufacturing process, allows employees to help create a better workplace for themselves and to improve the corporation. This book is a useful guide for equipping employees with the skills they need in a changing workplace, linking people and techniques to establish the company's competitive position in the market.

Jim Guzzo
Senior Consultant
Westinghouse Productivity & Quality Center

# Preface

The present era is not an easy one. The United States — source of economic aid for Japan during the early post-World War II era and leader in scientific business management centered on manufacturing technologies, quality control (QC), and industrial engineering (IE) — is grappling with high unemployment and other economic troubles. These tribulations have formed the backdrop for heated U.S. protests against Japan's supposed "dumping" of steel, automobiles, and other products.

Meanwhile, Japan has recovered so well from its wartime devastation that it now stands shoulder to shoulder with the United States and the leading European nations as an economic and technological superpower.

This trend has been met with a growing number of "boycott Japanese goods" movements in various countries. Japanese companies can no longer assume that their products can be exported and sold on their own merit in other countries. The overseas backlash against certain Japanese products has prompted Japan to apply the brakes on sensitive export items.

Domestically, Japan has had to bid farewell to its rapid-growth era and face a future devoid of such bullish expectations.

The road ahead is not clearly visible. Long ago, Japan's business leaders realized that if they can no longer put their trust in success based on quantity (mass production), they must turn to quality as the ticket to survival and prosperity. Japanese products sell well all over the world simply because they combine low cost with high quality.

Now Japanese industry has added a new angle to its pursuit of excellence in product quality: high added value. For example, Japan's automotive industry has developed a new type of corrosion-resistant car body sheet metal and other sheet metal that features superior chrome plating.

However, if high added value comes at too high a price, it will not sell. Therefore, companies have to strive constantly to keep costs down. Japanese companies have proved to be very good at this. Recently, other countries have begun to take note of the way Japanese companies have adopted American management techniques and developed them in their own way, under the banners of the TQC (total quality control) movement, QC circle activities, and, in the steel industry, autonomous management activities. These movements must be continuously developed to turn out better products and services. Japanese companies recognize the need to use QC and IE techniques in an endless succession of effective improvement activities.

This book is part of the *New Worksite QC Primer* series published by JUSE Press, and is one of four books based on IE-related themes.* You need not worry about what distinguishes QC from IE or how they relate to each other — remember only that both are management tools for building higher quality into products at lower cost.

---

* Productivity Press is publishing these four volumes as a set entitled *IE for the Shop Floor*; a translation of *Productivity Through Process Analysis* is available, and the other two volumes will follow in the future. — Ed.

This book explains the role of motion study as a means for promoting improvement activities. Inevitably, some of this book's discussion themes overlap with themes taken up in other books in this series. I have tried to describe motion study as simply and clearly as possible. If some parts of this explanation strike the reader as hard to understand, the blame must lie with myself and not with motion study, which need not be difficult.

Finally, I would like to offer my heartfelt gratitude to those who helped provide the improvement case studies that appear in the last chapter. I would also like to thank everyone at JUSE's publication offices for their kind assistance in producing this book.

Kenichirō Katō

# 1

# The Origins of IE: Frederick Taylor and Frank Gilbreth

IE (industrial engineering) is a familiar acronym to engineers and industrial managers in the United States, Japan, and elsewhere.

Although many people have studied and developed IE from a wide range of viewpoints, two individuals are widely recognized as its founders: Frederick W. Taylor (1856-1915) and Frank B. Gilbreth (1868-1924). Taylor is best known as the founder of scientific management and time study, and Gilbreth earned his fame as the creator of motion study.

Both of these men became famous in the 1880s for their work in observing the operations of workers under then-current "efficient supply" systems, establishing new operation methods and standard operation times, and thereby achieving higher productivity — which translated into higher wages for the workers. These new methods became known as the scientific management approach.

Both men pursued higher productivity as their main goal, both developed new IE techniques, and both put their methods to successful use. The fields of study that they founded were named according to their different approaches to the same goal. Taylor's field became known as *time study* or *work measurement,* and Gilbreth's field was called *motion study* or *methods engineering.*

Their approaches both rested upon the same scientific foundations: they observed the actual work done by actual workers at their worksite, refused to rely on intuition, and instead collected measurable data, which they subjected to scientific analysis leading to productivity-enhancing improvements. You need not concern yourself with the intricacies of their original approaches, but simply recognize them as the origins of modern IE.

The following sections describe some simple examples carried out by Taylor and Gilbreth.

## TAYLOR'S SHOVEL STUDY

Frederick Taylor performed this study in 1898 while working at Bethlehem Steel. Back then, iron ore and rice coal were conveyed almost completely by shovel. A typical job site included 400 to 600 manual laborers working with simple shovels. Some of the first things that Taylor noticed were that

- the better workers used their own shovels instead of the ones provided by the company,
- the foremen each had from 50 to 60 workers under their charge, and
- workers shoveled various types of ore or coal and moved around over a very large area.

Taylor's preliminary study showed that the average worker extracted 3.5 pounds of rice coal or 38 pounds of iron ore per day. He also took the largest daily output figure and calculated the load per shovel.

Using a stopwatch, Taylor timed and measured the amounts of coal and iron ore that the two best workers could produce in a day when using shovels in various sizes.

Taylor's most effective improvement was to establish a standard output value and to set up a reward system to pay bonuses to workers who surpass that standard value. At the same time, he observed and analyzed the work done by workers who consistently failed to meet the standard output value and helped them learn how to be more productive so that they too could start earning bonuses.

Three and a half years later, Taylor's efforts paid off for the company: A yield that used to require 400 to 600 men could now be produced by about 140 men and thereby reduced the company's cost of handling the material from seven or eight cents per ton to three or four cents per ton.

## GILBRETH'S STUDY OF BRICKLAYING MOTIONS

In the late nineteenth century, Frank Gilbreth worked for a building contractor. Brick construction was an important part of most structures at the time, and Gilbreth started out as an apprentice bricklayer.

Watching his fellow bricklayers, Gilbreth noticed that each one had his own methods of working. He also noticed, for example, that each worker might use three different sets of methods depending on what he was doing:

- One set for when he was working quickly
- Another set for when he was working slowly
- A third set for when he was teaching a less experienced worker how to lay bricks

These observations started Gilbreth wondering what the best way to do the work might be, and this put him on the road to motion study. He came up with several work method improvements and found that difficult, fatiguing motions could in many cases be replaced by simpler, less tiring ones.

For example, Gilbreth noticed that when bricklayers worked from a scaffold, they kept bricks stacked up on the scaffold floor and had to lean over to pick up each one. To lay the bricks, the bricklayers would select a brick from the stack, turn the brick or flip it over to find the best side for the wall face, then lay the brick onto the structure.

Gilbreth immediately understood that this method was both tiring and inefficient. He then decided to photograph the bricklayers at work and study their positions. He devised a way to place the scaffold at the most convenient height for laying the bricks and also installed a shelf on the scaffold so that the bricks and mortar could be stacked at a higher level, where they could be picked up with less effort and strain.

Gilbreth also noticed that the bricklayers needed only one hand to pick up and lay bricks, so he arranged the brick shelf and the mortar box so that the bricklayer could pick up a brick with one hand while getting a trowel full of mortar with the other hand. He also devised a way to keep the mortar at the proper consistency so that the bricklayer could just push the brick into place instead of tapping it in with the trowel.

Such improvements enabled Gilbreth to reduce the number of motions required to lay brick from 18 to just 4.5. As a result, bricklayers whom Gilbreth trained in these new methods managed to achieve an average rate of 350 bricks per hour while laying bricks on both sides of a 12-inch wall (a difficult bricklaying job). This was nearly triple the previous record of 120 bricks per hour.

In many motion study development projects, Frank Gilbreth worked with his wife Lillian, who was a psychologist. In fact, many consider Lillian Gilbreth to have contributed more to their work in production management than did her husband.

The Gilbreths rarely used the stopwatch method. Always looking for the very best work method, they aimed to find out how a job could be done in the minimum amount of time. This is why Frank Gilbreth preferred photography for motion analysis, using it in micromotion study, motion path study (using cyclegraphs and chronocyclegraphs), and other fields that he pioneered. Chapter 2 describes these types of motion study and introduces therblig analysis, a method devised by the Gilbreths for directly observing and analyzing work operations. (Therblig analysis is covered in more detail in Chapter 4.)

A full century ago, Taylor and the Gilbreths were developing IE methods and engaging in improvement activities that are still in use today and are central to the QC movement.

Making operations easier (less tiring), better (higher quality), cheaper (lower cost), and faster (more efficient) has always been an issue, not only in business activities but in every kind of productive activity. Taylor's main way of doing this was to clock the current work methods using a stopwatch, using time as a measure upon which to base improvements. The Gilbreths' main approach was to carefully watch a worker's movements, find ways to eliminate the Big 3 problems — waste, irrationality, and inconsistency — and make improvements that reduced the time required for the operations.

You are invited to follow in the footsteps of these improvement-minded trailblazers by using the stopwatch method and motion study to improve operations at your own workplace. In so doing, you will need to determine which IE method is best suited to your improvement needs. The more methods that people can suggest for a particular improvement, the better — as long as they are scientific methods and not intuitional ones. It does not matter if they are IE methods or QC methods; the important thing is that they make work easier, better, cheaper, and faster.

This book covers only one type of improvement method, motion study. This does not mean that motion study is the only or necessarily the best method to be used in each case. Nonetheless, it is fair to say that motion study lies at the root of operation improvement. This book will teach you how to use motion study to better understand the way you work.

# 2

# Motion and Motion Study

## WHAT IS MOTION?

Just looking at your everyday activities, you might notice the wide assortment of motions that you go through. For example, look at a typical pattern of activities that takes place when someone gets up in the morning and goes to work.

1. Get out of bed
2. Wash/shave or apply makeup
3. Get dressed
4. Read newspaper
5. Eat breakfast
6. Go to work

If you look more closely at just one of these activities, such as getting out of bed, you might note the following motions:

(a) Open eyes
(b) Stretch body
(c) Push off covers
(d) Get up

These motions can be subjected to even closer analysis, but this is close enough for now. You probably make these types of motions quite naturally and unconsciously as part of your daily routine. In motion analysis, these typical human actions and behaviors are viewed as combinations of discrete motions made by various parts of the body.

This same kind of motion study is used to study production activities. The three basic elements in production activities are

- man/woman
- machine
- material

These are called the "3Ms" (some people cite four basic elements, adding "method" to make "4Ms"). These basic elements can be found in any production activity (except in fully automated factories, where machine has replaced man and woman).

Just as with normal daily activities, production activities can also be broken down into combinations of specific motions. In other words, one can study the individual motions that come together as the job performance operations of factory workers.

## THE PURPOSE OF MOTION STUDY

Think about the three basic phases of the manufacturing business: buying materials, manufacturing products, and selling the products. To make the three M elements work together, you need to determine the specific processes, operations, and motions that are involved in making the products. In other words, operation standards are necessary.

Following the operation standards, workers use machines to process materials; hence there are production activities. As time passes, the workers gradually become so familiar with their work activities that these activities become as natural to them as the other routine activities that fill their days.

You must ask yourself, however, whether sticking with what comes naturally is good for the workers and the company in the long term. Other things happen over time, too. Material and labor costs rise with inflation. If the company hopes to counter inflation with lower costs instead of higher product prices, it must find ways to lower production costs and/or raise productivity. On top of that, the company should also look into simplifying its processes or upgrading them with new technologies. In other words, it must critically review its operation standards.

You might think it is a good thing that workers can become so accustomed to their work that it becomes a virtually subconscious process, like getting up in the morning. Actually, this is not the case.

Most workers who know their jobs very well come to regard their way of doing the job as "the natural way." However, if you analyze their activities closely enough to identify the combinations of motions that go into them, you will find ample room for improvement. For example, you will find the Big 3 problems — waste, irrationality, and inconsistency.* Improvement means rationalizing or simplifying the irrationality, smoothing inconsistencies and improving the work balance, and eliminating waste.

The possibility for improvement is infinite, which means you must constantly review how things are done and develop more efficient operation standards. Motion study is a set of techniques for improving work by observing and analyzing the actual motions that make up work operations.

---

* The Big 3 problem-finding framework is known in many Japanese factories as "three *mu*," after the Japanese names of its elements — *muda, mura,* and *muri* (waste, irrationality, and inconsistency). For more on the Big 3, see Tomo Sugiyama, *The Improvement Book* (Cambridge, Mass.: Productivity Press, 1989) and Japan Human Relations Association (ed.), *The Idea Book* (Cambridge, Mass.: Productivity Press, 1988) — Ed.

The purpose of motion study is threefold:

1. To understand motion sequences and methods in various parts of the operator's body
2. To clearly identify the Big 3 problems as they exist in these motions
3. To evaluate whether the operator is using his or her body in a balanced way to perform the work at hand

Take a look at an example of how motion study can be applied for a familiar type of work operation.

## A Motion Study Example: Modern Clothes Washing

As mentioned earlier, in motion study you will observe and analyze the motions that go into a work process. In this case — clothes washing — your analysis will focus primarily on the methods used.

Specifically, you will identify the left- and right-hand motions used when washing laundry (we call these motions "fundamental hand motions") and then tally them up and study them.

Today, washing clothes is usually a highly automated operation. Since most people own or have access to automatic washing machines, there is little to do by hand. However, back in the days of tubs and washboards, washing clothes was a big, time-consuming chore. Automatic washing machines were developed to do away with such work and allow people more time for other pursuits. When you automate anything, you should first study the manual way of doing it, then start devising ways to automate the manual work. This is probably how the developers of the first automatic washing machines proceeded.

This preliminary analysis of clothes-washing methods would definitely include some kind of motion and time study. However, in this case, we have the advantage of hindsight and can compare today's fully automatic washing machines with the old hand-washing method to find where improvements were made.

### Washing Clothes by Hand

In the old days, people used two main tools — a tub and a washboard — to hand-wash their clothes. Figure 2-1 illustrates these tools. Table 2-1 lists the left- and right-hand motions of the hand-washing process, as identified by a preliminary analysis.

### Washing Clothes Using a Fully Automatic Electric Washing Machine

Figure 2-2 shows the tools needed for modern-day clothes washing, in which one merely places a pile of laundry and some soap into a washing machine, then sets the switches to start the machine. This method of washing clothes has eliminated almost all of the manual work, as the analysis in Table 2-2 shows. Table 2-3 compares the results of the analyses listed in Tables 2-1 and 2-2.

As these tables show, analyzing the two clothes-washing methods gives us a quantitative measurement of the fundamental motions involved in each method. Naturally, the automatic washing machine method is much more rational (i.e., uses fewer fundamental motions) than the old manual method.

So far, you have seen one type of motion study. Note that this motion study method does not rely on "know-how" or "intuition," but instead uses quantitative, scientific methods to analyze operations and clearly understand their contents, making it easier to identify the Big 3 problems.

There are many other aspects of modern life that, like washing clothes, have become much easier. We now have cameras that automatically rewind the roll of film after it is finished, and there are wireless remote controls for televisions and stereos, automobiles with built-in computer circuits, and so on. Most of us take for granted the many electrical appliances that make

**Figure 2-1. The Old Way of Washing Clothes**

**Figure 2-2. Tools for Modern Clothes Washing**

housekeeping so much easier, but the fact is that they represent a revolution in housekeeping rationalization.

Every automated device that we enjoy today was developed via a process of operation analysis and elimination of Big 3 problems, which resulted in a major savings of time and labor. As such, these products are born of efforts to improve labor-related motions. Table 2-4 shows an outline of the labor improvements made by a few of today's more common automated devices.

## Table 2-1.  Analysis of Manual Clothes Washing Method

|  |  | Left Hand | Right Hand |
|---|---|---|---|
| Set up tub (4 motions) | 1 | Get tub<br>Extend arms toward tub | Get tub<br>Extend arms toward tub |
|  | 2 | Pick up tub | Pick up tub |
|  | 3 | Carry tub to washing place | Carry tub to washing place |
|  | 4 | Set tub down at washing place | Set tub down at washing place |
| Pour water into tub (12 motions) | 5 |  | Extend hand toward faucet handle |
|  | 6 |  | Grasp handle |
|  | 7 |  | Turn handle to release water |
|  | 8 |  | Remove hand from handle |
|  | 9* |  | Same as step 5 |
|  | 10 |  | Same as step 6 |
|  | 11 |  | Same as step 7 |
|  | 12 |  | Same as step 8 |
|  | 13 |  | Same as step 5 |
|  | 14 |  | Same as step 6 |
|  | 15 |  | Same as step 7 |
|  | 16 |  | Same as step 8 |
| Set up washboard (4 motions) | 17 |  | Get washboard<br>Extend arm toward washboard |
|  | 18 |  | Pick up washboard |
|  | 19 |  | Carry washboard to washing place |
|  | 20 |  | Put washboard down at washing place |

* Two rinse stages

**Table 2-1. (Continued)**

|  |  | Left Hand | Right Hand |
|---|---|---|---|
| Prepare laundry (4 motions) | 21 |  | Get laundry from hamper<br>Extend arm toward hamper |
|  | 22 |  | Pick up laundry |
|  | 23 |  | Carry laundry to washing place |
|  | 24 |  | Put laundry into tub |
| Prepare soap (4 motions) | 25 |  | Extend arm toward soap (go get soap) |
|  | 26 |  | Pick up soap |
|  | 27 |  | Carry soap to washing place |
|  | 28 |  | Put soap down |
| Turn off water (12 motions) | 29 |  | Extend arm toward faucet handle |
|  | 30 |  | Grasp handle |
|  | 31 |  | Turn handle to shut off water |
|  | 32 |  | Remove hand from handle |
|  | 33* |  | Same as step 29 |
|  | 34 |  | Same as step 30 |
|  | 35 |  | Same as step 31 |
|  | 36 |  | Same as step 32 |
|  | 37 |  | Same as step 29 |
|  | 38 |  | Same as step 30 |
|  | 39 |  | Same as step 31 |
|  | 40 |  | Same as step 32 |

* Two rinse stages

**Table 2-1. (Continued)**

|  |  | Left Hand | Right Hand |
|---|---|---|---|
| Wash clothes (24 motions) | 41 | Crouch down and extend arm toward washboard | Crouch down and extend arm toward washboard |
|  | 42 | Grasp washboard | Grasp washboard |
|  | 43 | Set washboard into correct position | Set washboard into correct position |
|  | 44 | Remove hand from washboard | Remove hand from washboard |
|  | 45 | Extend arm toward laundry in tub | Reach for soap |
|  | 46 | Pick up one piece of laundry | Pick up soap |
|  | 47 | Lift piece of laundry up to washboard | Lift soap to washboard |
|  | 48 | Hold piece of laundry on washboard | Rub soap onto piece of laundry (3 times) |
|  | 49 | Same as step 48 | Same as step 48 |
|  | 50 | " | Same as step 48 |
|  | 51 | " | Move soap back to soap tray |
|  | 52 | " | Remove hand from soap |
|  | 53 | " | Extend arm toward piece of laundry on washboard |
|  | 54 | " | Grasp piece of laundry |
|  | 55 | " | Scrub piece of laundry against washboard (10 times) |
|  | 56 | " | " |
|  | 57 | " | " |
|  | 58 | " | " |
|  | 59 | " | " |
|  | 60 | " | " |
|  | 61 | " | " |
|  | 62 | " | " |
|  | 63 | " | " |
|  | 64 | " | " |

**Table 2-2. Analysis of Automated Clothes Washing Method**

| | | Left Hand | Right Hand |
|---|---|---|---|
| Set up washing machine (8 motions) | 1 | | Go to washing machine and reach for dial |
| | 2 | | Grasp dial |
| | 3 | | Turn dial to START position |
| | 4 | | Remove hand from dial |
| | 5 | | Reach for water temperature switch |
| | 6 | | Grasp switch |
| | 7 | | Set switch to desired position |
| | 8 | | Remove hand from switch |
| Prepare laundry (6 motions) | 9 | | Get laundry from hamper (reach for laundry) |
| | 10 | | Grasp laundry |
| | 11 | Reach for lid of washing machine | Carry laundry to washing machine |
| | 12 | Grasp lid | |
| | 13 | Open lid | |
| | 14 | Remove hand from lid | Drop laundry into machine |
| Prepare detergent (6 motions) | 15 | | Get detergent (reach for detergent box) |
| | 16 | | Grasp detergent box |
| | 17 | Reach for lid of washing machine | Carry detergent to washing machine |
| | 18 | Grasp lid | Pour detergent into machine |
| | 19 | Shut lid | Carry detergent box back to where it was |
| | 20 | Remove hand from lid | Remove hand from detergent box |

**Table 2-3. Comparison of Manual and Automatic Clothes Washing Methods**

| Manual Clothes Washing Method | | Automatic Clothes Washing Method | | Difference in No. of Motions |
|---|---|---|---|---|
| Operation | Fundamental Motions | Operation | Fundamental Motions | |
| Set up tub | 4 | — | — | −4 |
| Pour water | 12 | Set dial | 8 | −4 |
| Set up washboard | 4 | — | — | −4 |
| Prepare laundry | 4 | Prepare laundry | 6 | +2 |
| Set up soap | 4 | Prepare detergent | 6 | +2 |
| Turn off faucet | 12 | — | — | −12 |
| Wash one piece of laundry | 24 | Wash one load of laundry | — | −24 |
| **Total** | **64** | | **20** | **−44** |

## TYPES OF MOTION STUDY

The old-fashioned clothes-washing example just given is an example of a manual operation that centered on the use of both hands. In general, work operations can be divided into those that require use of the whole body and those that mainly require use of only part of the body — usually the arms and hands. Moving goods between operations tends to belong to the former category, while assembly work tends to belong to the latter category.

When analyzing current conditions in work operations, you will sometimes start with a general observation and then follow up with a more detailed observation and analysis of parts of the operations that appear to require more attention.

There are various types of motion study to choose from, some suited to large operations and others to small ones. When using motion study, use the study method that provides the required degree of precision and that otherwise best suits the

**Table 2-4. Rationalization of Household Appliances**

| Operation | Product | Method | | Effects |
|---|---|---|---|---|
| | | **Old** | **New** | |
| Rice cooking | Electric rice cooker | Stand by to tend fire under rice pot (turn down flame after boiling; never lift the lid) | Set timer and go away | • Easier (not tiring)<br>• No inconsistency (standardized cooking temperature)<br>• No mistakes (easy operation)<br>• No waste of time (operates independently) |
| Clothes washing | Automatic washing machine | Scrub clothes using washboard, soap, and tub of water | Put a load of laundry and detergent into machine, then set switches | • No irrationality (easy to do)<br>• No waste of time (operates independently)<br>• No mistakes (easy operation)<br>• No inconsistency (can wash clothes in any weather) |
| Sweeping | Vacuum cleaner | Sweep using duster and broom | Turn switch to activate vacuum cleaner | • No inconsistency (picks up dust consistently)<br>• More efficient (does not kick up dust)<br>• Healthier to use (does not kick up dust) |
| Cold storage for food and beverages | Electric refrigerator | Put food and beverages in wells or rivers for cooling | Put food and beverages in refrigerator | • No waste (better storage)<br>• Better tasting food and beverages |
| Cooking | Microwave oven | Put food into stove-top pot or oven to cook it gradually | Put food into microwave oven and set switches | • No waste (saves time and energy)<br>• Less risk of mistakes<br>• No inconsistency |

operation being studied. A very basic breakdown of motion study types would include the following four methods:

- Operator process analysis
- Therblig analysis
- Film analysis
- Cyclegraphic and chronocyclegraphic analysis

Each of these methods has different features and is oriented toward different objectives. For example, you might wish to begin your study of a production process by conducting a motion study using operator process analysis to gain a general understanding of the production process and its problems. You could then use therblig analysis to zero in on specific problems. The next sections show how you might go about this.

## Motion Study Using Operator Process Analysis

Product process analysis is an IE technique that we can use to study how materials, parts, and products move among various processes. This type of analysis is described in detail in Junichi Ishiwata's *IE for the Shop Floor : Productivity Through Process Analysis* (Cambridge, Ma.: Productivity Press, 1991). The process chart symbols used for product process analysis are similar to those used for *operator process analysis,* which aims to study the motions of operators (workers). Table 2-5 lists these symbols and the categories of factory operations that they represent.

Operations can mean physically or chemically altering the shape or contents of something, assembling or taking apart components, or other productive work. Transportation, or conveyance, means moving objects from one place to another. Inspection can mean checking things to make sure they meet standards, or counting and weighing to check for the required quantity and weight. Delays, or standby, can mean idle workers or idle equipment; in either case it means a period of no productive work. Delays should be eliminated as much as possible through improvement of the operation methods.

**Table 2-5. Operator Process Analysis Symbols**

| Category | Symbol |
|---|---|
| Operation | ○ |
| Transportation | ○ <br> (⇨) |
| Inspection | □ |
| Delay (Standby) | ▽ <br> (D) |

### *Operator Process Analysis*

Here is an example of how to use the process chart symbols for operations (large circle), transportation (small circle or arrow), inspection (square), and delays (triangle). Figure 2-3 shows a simple factory layout diagram; the first floor is the operations and inspection area and the second floor is the parts storage area.

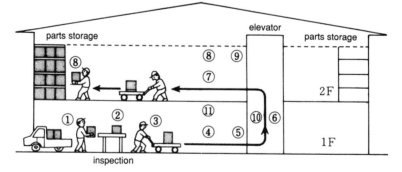

**Figure 2-3. Factory Layout Diagram**

Table 2-6 is the process chart recording the process symbols for this factory's series of activities. Looking at these analysis results, you might note the two delays (steps 5 and 10 in

Table 2-6) and consider moving the parts storage shelves to the first floor. This would eliminate the delays, shorten the transportation distance, and do away with the time spent using the elevators.

**Table 2-6. Sample Operator Process Chart — Parts Acceptance Operations**

| No. | Description | Operation | Transport | Delays | Inspection | Time (min.) | Distance (m) |
|---|---|---|---|---|---|---|---|
| 1 | Unload parts from truck onto inspection table | ● | ○ | ▽ | □ | 5 | |
| 2 | Inspect parts | ○ | ○ | ▽ | ■ | ~ 30 | |
| 3 | Load nondefective parts onto cart | ● | ○ | ▽ | □ | 5 | |
| 4 | Push cart to elevator | ○ | ● | ▽ | □ | 2 | ~ 20 |
| 5 | Wait for elevator | ○ | ○ | ▼ | □ | 1 | |
| 6 | Go to second floor in elevator | ○ | ● | ▽ | □ | 1 | |
| 7 | Push cart out of elevator to parts storage shelves | ○ | ● | ▽ | □ | 2 | ~ 20 |
| 8 | Load parts onto parts storage shelves | ● | ○ | ▽ | □ | 5 | |
| 9 | Push empty cart back to elevator | ○ | ● | ▽ | □ | 2 | ~ 20 |
| 10 | Wait for elevator | ○ | ○ | ▼ | □ | 1 | |
| 11 | Return to first floor in elevator | ○ | ● | ▽ | □ | 1 | |
| 12 | Return cart and self to original positions | ○ | ● | ▽ | □ | 2 | ~ 20 |
| | No. of steps | 3 | 6 | 2 | 1 | 57 | ~ 80 |

You could go on with further improvement suggestions, but for now, stop here and note how even a very basic operator process analysis can give quantitative measurements of processes, operation times, and distances. These make it much easier to see where layout improvements can be made to reduce the number of processes and, most important, to minimize transportation and delays.

### Steps in Operator Process Analysis

*Step 1: Determine the purpose of the analysis.* Within the framework of motion study, your purpose is usually related to raising the efficiency of operations, but sometimes it can be for another purpose, such as improving the layout.

*Step 2: Select a target operator who has learned the new operations well and is of average ability.*

*Step 3: Determine the scope of operations to be analyzed.* Usually, it is better to define the scope as one cycle of operations (such as a cycle composed of 12 steps), then do a general analysis. After the general analysis, you can see where a more detailed analysis might be needed within the cycle.

*Step 4: Observe the operations.* If necessary, interview the operators about what they are doing until you fully understand what is going on in those operations.

*Step 5: Create or obtain process chart forms and fill them in with your observations.*

*Step 6: Determine how detailed the analysis should be.* Begin by matching up descriptions of the steps with the process chart symbols. For example, for drilling a hole in the part with a drilling machine, you would use an operation symbol (large circle). Moving the workpiece before and after the operation would be transportation (small circle or arrow).

Of course, these descriptions are very general and could easily be made more specific. For example, "pick up part" could be broken down into "reach for part," "grasp part," "set up part on drilling machine," and so on. You will use this level of detail when you begin using therblig analysis, but it is better to stay at a general level of analysis for the operator process analysis stage. As you will see later on (in an analysis of work done with both hands), these process chart symbols can be used for detailed operation descriptions, too.

*Step 7: Create an operator process chart.* Once you have drawn up an operator process chart, you can see whether the main problem concerns excess transportation distance (in which case, take a closer look at the layout of operations) or excess operation time (in which case, focus on time measurements). Using your data chart, you can tally the number of symbols used and thereby determine whether the cycle contains an excess of transportation or delays.

*Step 8: Draft improvement plans and create an improvement plan process chart.* In making improvements, the important thing is to discover why each delay or transportation step is there. Quite often the improvement requires a new layout design. You also need to ask why each processing and inspection step is necessary, so that you might find ways of streamlining them.

*Step 9: Decide on an improvement plan, implement the plan, and verify the results.*

### Example of Two-handed Operation Analysis

Earlier, an example was given for how to use process analysis symbols to make a general analysis of parts acceptance operations at a factory. Here, the same symbols will be used to make a somewhat more detailed analysis.

In manual operations, you often run into delay (standby) points, and you also frequently encounter points where one hand is idle (or is just holding an object) while the other hand is performing an operation. Since simply holding an object is something between being idle and working, you use a special symbol (double triangle) to represent this holding operation when analyzing two-handed work.

Figure 2-4 shows the layout for a two-handed operation for assembling nuts and bolts. Table 2-7 shows the process chart for this two-handed nut-and-bolt assembly operation, and Table 2-8 shows the corresponding data chart.

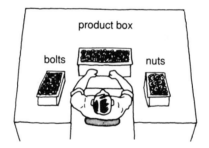

**Figure 2-4. Operation Layout Diagram (Before Improvement)**

In this example, the layout diagram (Figure 2-4) shows the bolt box and nut box on either side of the operator. This means that the operator must look toward whichever box he or she is picking up a part from. Specifically:

- To pick up a bolt, the operator looks to the left and reaches with the left hand.
- To pick up a nut, the operator looks to the right and reaches with the right hand.

The fact that the operator must look in either direction means that he or she must first pick up one part and then hold that part while picking up the other part.

## Table 2-7. Two-handed Process Chart (Before Improvement)

| No. | Motion | Left Hand ◯ ○ □ ▽ ▽ | | | | | Right Hand ▽ ▽ □ ○ ◯ | | | | | Motion |
|-----|--------|---|---|---|---|---|---|---|---|---|---|--------|
| 1 | Reach for bolt | ◯ | ○ | □ | ▽ | ▽ | ▽ | ▽ | □ | ○ | ◯ | Standby |
| 2 | Grasp bolt | ◯ | ○ | □ | ▽ | ▽ | ▽ | ▽ | □ | ○ | ◯ | " |
| 3 | Move bolt to assembly site (above product box) | ◯ | ○ | □ | ▽ | ▽ | ▽ | ▽ | □ | ○ | ◯ | " |
| 4 | Hold bolt | ◯ | ○ | □ | ▽ | ▽ | ▽ | ▽ | □ | ○ | ◯ | Reach for nut |
| 5 | " | ◯ | ○ | □ | ▽ | ▽ | ▽ | ▽ | □ | ○ | ◯ | Grasp nut |
| 6 | " | ◯ | ○ | □ | ▽ | ▽ | ▽ | ▽ | □ | ○ | ◯ | Move nut to assembly site |
| 7 | Line up bolt with nut | ◯ | ○ | □ | ▽ | ▽ | ▽ | ▽ | □ | ○ | ◯ | Line up nut with bolt |
| 8 | Hold bolt | ◯ | ○ | □ | ▽ | ▽ | ▽ | ▽ | □ | ○ | ◯ | Screw nut onto bolt |
| 9 | Remove hand | ◯ | ○ | □ | ▽ | ▽ | ▽ | ▽ | □ | ○ | ◯ | Remove hand |

## Table 2-8. Data Chart (Before Improvement)

| | Left Hand | Right Hand |
|---|---|---|
| Operation ◯ | 2 | 3 |
| Transport ○ | 3 | 3 |
| Inspection □ | — | — |
| Standby ▽ | — | 3 |
| Hold ▽ | 4 | — |
| Total | 9 | 9 |

You might improve this operation by enabling the operator to pick up both parts at the same time. To do this, simply move the bolt and nut boxes forward on the work table, as shown in Figure 2-5, so that they are both within the operator's field of vision when he or she looks straight ahead. Now that the operator can see both parts boxes at once, he or she can reach for them both at once.

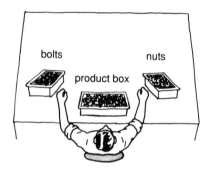

**Figure 2-5. Operation Layout Diagram (After Improvement)**

Table 2-9 shows the process chart describing this new layout, and Table 2-10 shows the corresponding data organization chart. The data chart shows that the improvement has eliminated three motions for each hand.

In this example, the transformation of sequential two-handed operations into simultaneous two-handed operations is given as one type of operation improvement. This type of improvement is not possible for some types of sequential two-handed operations, as will be explained later on.

In the above example, the improvement involved shifting the positions of the parts boxes to within the operator's normal or optimum work area. This is the work area within which the operator can move most economically, with minimum waste, irrationality, and inconsistency. Using the normal work area

**Table 2-9. Two-handed Process Chart (After Improvement)**

| No. | Motion | Left Hand ○ ○ □ ▽ ▽ | Right Hand ▽ ▽ □ ○ ○ | Motion |
|-----|--------|-----------|-----------|--------|
| 1 | Reach for bolt | ○ ○ □ ▽ ▽ | ▽ ▽ □ ○ ○ | Reach for nut |
| 2 | Grasp bolt | ○ ○ □ ▽ ▽ | ▽ ▽ □ ○ ○ | Grasp nut |
| 3 | Move bolt to product box | ○ ○ □ ▽ ▽ | ▽ ▽ □ ○ ○ | Move nut to product box |
| 4 | Line up bolt with nut | ○ ○ □ ▽ ▽ | ▽ ▽ □ ○ ○ | Line up nut with bolt |
| 5 | Hold bolt | ○ ○ □ ▽ ▽ | ▽ ▽ □ ○ ○ | Screw nut onto bolt |
| 6 | Remove hand (drop product into product box) | ○ ○ □ ▽ ▽ | ▽ ▽ □ ○ ○ | Remove hand (drop product into product box) |

**Table 2-10. Data Chart (After Improvement)**

| | Left Hand | Right Hand |
|---|---|---|
| Operation ○ | 2 | 3 |
| Transport ○ | 3 | 3 |
| Inspection □ | — | — |
| Standby ▽ | — | — |
| Hold ▽ | 1 | — |
| Total | 6 | 6 |

concept in designing the work area is one of the principles of motion economy, an important set of tools in motion study. Chapter 4 provides a closer look at how changing the positions of the parts boxes in this example follows the principles of motion economy.

## Therblig Analysis

Operator process analysis is well suited for gaining a basic understanding of operations; *therblig analysis* is a tool better suited to more detailed studies. Operator process analysis generally uses just 4 main categories (operations, transportation, inspection, and delay) to break down its observations. Therblig analysis, in comparison, uses 18 categories to facilitate a much more detailed analysis.

These categories and their symbols are sometimes referred to as "therbligs." They were invented by Frank Gilbreth, who coined the word as a reverse spelling of his own name. Today, virtually everyone who performs motion study uses these therblig symbols or their letter equivalents. The topic of therblig analysis using these symbols will be taken up in detail in Chapter 4.

## Film Analysis

The human eye has a limited ability to observe and analyze motion. To take an example from baseball, it is very difficult to observe and study the exact form of a fastball pitch. Baseball coaches cannot simply watch a pitcher throw a fastball and see where the angle of pitch or the pitcher's grasp on the ball might need improvement, since the pitcher's arm becomes a blur to the eye.

That is where *film analysis* comes to the rescue. If the pitcher's motion is filmed with high-speed film, both he and the coach will be able to later observe the form of the pitch in slow motion, analyzing each stage of motion in the pitch. Likewise, film analysis also serves as a valuable tool for improving fast or very precise motions in production activities.

Time-lapse photography (using slow film) is another important method in film analysis, and is especially effective for studying the motions of workers who move over a large work area. The accelerated sequence of motions that time-lapse photography produces makes it easier to see which parts of the work area are being used the most and where the wasteful motions are.

### Memomotion Study

Memomotion study is the least detailed type of micromotion study, usually using a relatively slow film exposure speed (60 to 100 frames per minute). The finished film is projected at normal speed for analysis. The result is a choppy sequence of motions, reminiscent of the early silent movies.

Memomotion study is most commonly used in the following types of situations:

1. If the operation cycle is at least two minutes long and if it need not be observed at full motion (such as the movies shown in cinemas), memomotion study can save film costs.
2. Memomotion study is also effective when one operation cycle is very long. The person analyzing the process can save time by observing the memomotion pictures instead of the "live" operations.
3. Memomotion is good to use when there are many people carrying out operations on the same floor in the factory. Memomotion makes it easier to see how the operators' motions interrelate.

### Regular Film Analysis

Although memomotion study is one type of film analysis, the original purpose of film analysis was to make visible the minute and/or rapid motions that the eye is too slow to catch. Regular film analysis uses a film exposure rate of at least 16 frames per second; the finished film is projected one frame at a time to analyze each swift stage of motion.

Since shooting at 16 frames or more per second uses a lot of film, this type of analysis is generally reserved for the following situations: very brief operation cycles, very repetitive motions, or operation methods used for mass production. This method sometimes requires very fast film, shooting at speeds of 24, 32, or even 64 frames per second. Recently, video recording has come into widespread use as a cost-saving alternative to conventional cinematographic methods.

## Cyclegraphic and Chronocyclegraphic Analyses

These two techniques are useful for studying very short, repetitive motions and for studying the motion paths taken by certain parts of the body, usually the hands.

In *cyclegraphic analysis*, a small electric light bulb is attached to the operator's target body part (such as on a finger). The operator is then filmed from three angles (front, side, and top). The photos will show streaks of light describing the paths of motion, as recorded by the three cameras.

*Chronocyclegraphic analysis* uses a light bulb that blinks at steady intervals. This produces photos of motion paths described by comet-shaped dots. The comet "tails" indicate the direction of motion, and their space intervals indicate the speed of each motion.

Cyclegraphic and chronocyclegraphic methods are used mostly for academic purposes, but they occasionally find practical application for studying swift, repetitive operations.

# 3

# Motion Study Goals and Steps

## THE GOAL OF MOTION STUDY:
## TO ELIMINATE THE BIG 3 PROBLEMS

Chapter 2 presented examples of operator process analysis (parts acceptance operations at a factory) and of two-hand operation analysis (clothes washing and bolt/nut assembly operations). Those examples showed how motion study can reveal where the *Big 3 problems* (irrationality, inconsistency, and waste) exist in operations performed by people. This chapter will consider another concrete example, this time relating to transportation activities.

Figure 3-1 shows two ways of conveying heavy loads of products, by hand and by cart. First consider hand conveyance. As the picture shows, it often means a strain on the worker, not to mention the risk of injury if any of the boxes should fall. For safety reasons alone, one should do everything possible to avoid this irrational risk. Even putting aside safety concerns, carrying such heavy loads will soon take its toll on the worker's endurance, and there will be inconsistency as the increasingly tired worker takes longer and longer to carry them to their destination. This irrationality and inconsistency can be eliminated effectively if a cart or forklift is used to move the product loads. Since this improvement would also mean a faster conveyance time, it eliminates time-related waste, too (see Figure 3-1).

**Figure 3-1. Transportation**

This example analyzes the current way of doing things, identifies the Big 3 problems that exist, and devises an improvement to eliminate them and also make  the work easier and more efficient. This is the ideal approach to take, similar to the methods of the founders of industrial engineering a century ago. The ultimate goal is to make your work more enjoyable and productive.

Think a little more about the attitude and approach that you bring to work every day. The first thing you need is a critical eye. You should wonder, Why are we doing things this way? With this in mind, take one more look at how this attitude might relate to the load-carrying example.

1. First ask why the transportation is necessary at all and what would happen if it were eliminated.
2. You realize that eliminating the transportation would provide an opportunity for more closely linking the previous and subsequent production processes.

3. When you look at how this might work in practical terms, you discover that establishing a direct link between the two processes or combining the processes would require too large an investment in equipment. You begin to wonder if there might be a cheaper alternative.
4. You decide that since you cannot cheaply eliminate the transportation process, you will instead change the process to make it more efficient. This is where you come up with the idea of using carts instead of carrying the loads by hand.

The important thing to note here is not the improvement idea itself (using carts) but rather the steps by which you arrived at the idea. You begin by questioning the need for the entire transportation process and looking for a way to eliminate it altogether. This is the kind of critical attitude to use in observing current operating conditions. Your primary intention should be to eliminate the Big 3 problems. Figure 3-2 illustrates this process of elimination.

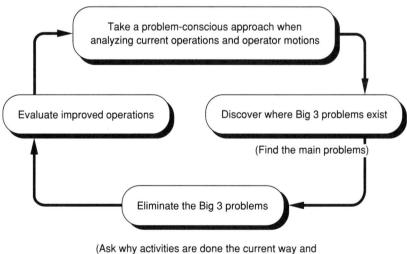

**Figure 3-2. Steps in Eliminating the Big 3 Problems**

When studying current conditions, you can also refer to a Big 3 discovery checklist, such as the one shown in Table 3-1, and a list of the four improvement principles, as shown in Table 3-2.

**Table 3-1.  Big 3 Problem Discovery Checklist**
**(Human Operations and Motions)**

| Problem | Check point | Checkoff | |
| --- | --- | --- | --- |
| | | YES | NO |
| Irrationality | • Are any of the motions irrational? | | |
| | • Are any of the work postures irrational? | | |
| | • Is there anything in the workplace environment that makes for irrational operations? | | |
| | • Can the operations be made easier? | | |
| | • Are any of the operations unsafe? | | |
| | • Is the arrangement of worker stations irrational? | | |
| | • Can the staffing be reduced? | | |
| Inconsistency | • Is there much variation in the operation methods? | | |
| | • Do different operators have their own ways of doing things? | | |
| | • Is there variation in the workload among operators? | | |
| | • Do different people have different output levels and speeds? | | |
| | • Do the operators work well together? | | |
| Waste | • Are there any wasteful motions? (standby or idle time, etc.) | | |
| | • Are any of the operations overdone (such as inspection)? | | |
| | • Are the workers positioned in a wasteful arrangement? | | |
| | • Is work assigned in a wasteful manner? | | |
| | • Is waste created by poor planning or poor changeover operations? | | |

**Table 3-2. The Four Improvement Principles**

| | Principle | Hints | Applications |
|---|---|---|---|
| 1 | Eliminate | 1. Get rid of wasteful factors<br>2. Eliminate unnecessary work }Why are things being done this way? | • Eliminating unnecessary external appearance inspections<br>• Linking processes to eliminate conveyance |
| 2 | Combine | 1. Consolidate operations<br>2. Combine operations<br>3. Make sequential operations simultaneous | • Soldering several points at the same process<br>• Combining stamp with ink pad<br>• Inspecting while processing |
| 3 | Rearrange | 1. Change the sequence of operations<br>2. Replace one way of doing something with another way<br>3. Replace one object with another | • Moving the inspection process upstream<br>• Using carts instead of hand-carrying<br>• Replacing the materials |
| 4 | Simplify | 1. Make things simpler<br>2. Make things easier<br>3. Reduce quantities | • Eliminating unneeded functions<br>• Lightening the workload<br>• Standardizing parts to reduce variety |

It bears repeating that the starting point should always be the first improvement principle: eliminate. Always ask, Why are we doing things this way and what would happen if we eliminated such-and-such an operation? Only when you know why an operation cannot be completely eliminated should you begin to look for ways to improve it — by simplifying, combining, or changing the sequence of things (the other three improvement principles).

Refer again to the cycle of steps shown in Figure 3-2. Also look at Figure 3-3, which embodies a somewhat broader description of the same cycle. The management cycle shown in Figure 3-3 is an expanded version of the PDCA (plan-do-check-action) cycle, familiar to many people from the QC movement. As an improvement-minded person, you should have this cycle turning through your thoughts as you confront problems in production operations.

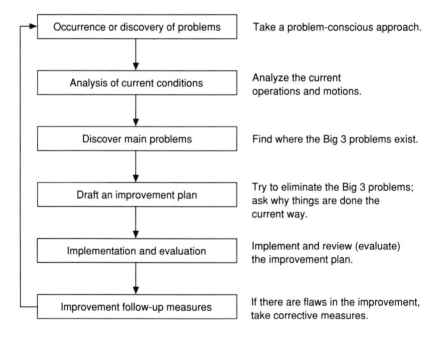

**Figure 3-3. The Management Cycle**

## STEPS IN WORK IMPROVEMENTS: AROUND AND AROUND THE PDCA CYCLE

The goals of motion improvements are to study how motion is being done, find where the Big 3 problems exist, then eliminate them to make operations easier, better, faster, and cheaper.

The cycle in Figure 3-3 is the management cycle for making such improvements. This cycle is not something that you do once and then stop. After you have improved a situation, that situation becomes the "current condition" to be critically evaluated as the starting point for another improvement cycle. Thus, you go around and around this management cycle, making one motion improvement after another. In this chapter you will look at each step in the management cycle and see what needs to be done at each step to keep the cycle going.

## Discover the Problem

Problems will come to your attention in one of two ways. One is when a problem just suddenly occurs. The other way is when you discover a potential problem before it becomes obvious. You do this by paying close daily attention to measurable factors such as efficiency, capacity utilization, yield, and unit costs, so that things do not suddenly take a turn for the worse. It is only when little attention is paid that problems seem to appear out of the blue.

Since dealing with abnormalities only after they have become true problems is doing too little too late, the wiser course is to analyze conditions while the inherent problems are still minor and to deal with problems then, while they are still relatively easy to solve.

Remember always to look at your current situation with a critical eye. This means you must collect data on current conditions as you make daily inspection rounds so that you can discover the small problems before they become large ones. It is useful to have a checklist such as the one shown in Table 3-3, to look for all the checkpoints. (This particular checklist is called PQCDSM, from the initials of the main check items listed in the table.)

The term "motion-minded" was coined to describe the attitude of people who have learned how to constantly look with a

**Table 3-3. PQCDSM Checklist**

| Check Item | Check Point (example) |
|---|---|
| Productivity (P) | • Has the output decreased lately? |
| Quality (Q) | • Has quality declined recently?<br>• Has the defect rate risen?<br>• Have the number of customer complaints risen? |
| Cost (C) | • Have costs risen?<br>• Have yield, efficiency, capacity utilization, or unit cost worsened?<br>• Are too many workers being used? |
| Delivery (D) | • Have deliveries been late? |
| Safety (S) | • Have there been any safety problems?<br>• Have the number of accidents or injuries risen?<br>• Are any current operations unsafe? |
| Morale (M) | • Do people have a positive attitude toward their work?<br>• Are there any interpersonal problems?<br>• Have the workers been assigned appropriate jobs? |

critical eye at the motions made in production activities, and who continually ask themselves, Why is that motion necessary? and, Can it be made easier to do?

## Analyze Current Conditions

As soon as you get some indication that a problem is developing, you need to make a thorough study of the relevant conditions. The most popular method for doing such a study is the 5W1H (5 Whys & 1 How) method, described in the checklist in Table 3-4. After making such an investigation, it becomes much easier to understand what the current conditions are. As any journalist knows, the 5W1H method of inquiry is a powerful tool for getting to the bottom of the story.

**Table 3-4. 5W1H Checklist**

| Item | Question (5W1H) |
|---|---|
| Target | What is done? |
| Operator | Who is doing it? |
| Purpose | Why is it done? |
| Place/position | Where is it done? |
| Time/period | When is it done? |
| Method | How is it done? |

Nothing else in the PDCA cycle can compare to this method in terms of its ability to reveal the facts about current conditions. There is no substitute for seeing what is going on with your own eyes and writing down your firsthand observations.

At the risk of repetition, turn back to the matter of the attitude you bring to your study of current conditions. This attitude should take the following manifestations:

- Study the facts as they are
- Be objective
- Express the facts in quantitative terms
- Use symbols and charts

### Study the Facts as They Are

When studying current conditions, avoid making any hasty criticisms or suppositions about the way things are being done. Instead, simply stick to the facts: find out how operator A is doing the work, what the work involves, why the work is needed, where it is being done, and when it must be done.

Most of all, avoid the temptation to make predictions and estimations of the conditions without observing them firsthand at the workplace.

### Be Objective

Studying the facts as they are requires objectivity. If you allow your own opinions or preferences to influence your interpretation of the facts, you will obviously not gain a clear and accurate understanding of the current conditions. If the person analyzing the current conditions suspects that he or she cannot be objective (perhaps because the conditions include those at his or her own job), a disinterested third party should be found to do the analysis.

The most effective way to carry out motion study is to use the various tools developed for studying conditions in the workplace. These tools include the process analysis and two-hand operation analysis methods that were explained in Chapter 2, along with the therbligs that will be explained in

Chapter 4. The important thing is to render the facts clear enough for anyone to understand easily.

Once you have obtained the facts about the current conditions, you can use the well-known seven QC tools, such as cause-and-effect diagrams, to objectively look into the causes of those conditions.

### Express the Facts in Quantitative Terms

The next requirement is to make sure that even the tiniest bits of data are expressed in quantitative, measurable terms instead of qualitative, intuitive ones. It is much easier to identify the problem points and to set priorities when the facts are expressed in measurable figures. If you do not bother to measure and record such figures but just write "the operations are too slow" or "the quality is getting worse," it becomes very difficult to make correct judgments about what improvements are needed.

In QC activities, circle members are always drawing up charts (i.e., Pareto charts, histograms, and other tools) to assist their analysis and evaluation of current conditions. Data are the basic material out of which these diagrams are made. Not just any data will do — they must be quantitative data. Good data constitute the key for finding problems and working out well-focused improvements.

### Use Symbols and Charts

Once you have quantitative data, you can use them to create charts and tables. If you use symbols to indicate certain types of operations or motions, the charts will become easier to read and understand. Visual symbols and diagrams speak more directly to the mind and are easier to compare than words and sentences, and therefore they are more persuasive. This is why the Pareto chart, for example, has become such a familiar and popular tool in QC activities.

In applying these four principles, it might be helpful to consider, as a model, the manner in which a detective investigates the scene of the crime.

1. Leaving the place just as it was when the crime was committed, the detective makes a thorough investigation in an objective manner.
2. The detective takes photos of the place and draws diagrams showing the layout of its main contents (perhaps using special symbols or graphs).
3. The detective collects as much physical evidence as possible and makes quantitative descriptions of each item.
4. The detective then questions everyone who works or lives nearby in an attempt to solve the mysteries of the case.

In improvement activities and in motion study, you will be almost exactly like a detective investigating a crime, proceeding rationally and scientifically toward its solution. When you go to the "scene of the crime" to investigate, your report should include facts such as

- the names of the materials
- the quantities being used
- the time required for the operations
- the method of doing the operations
- the names of the machines being used
- the positions and uses of containers

Show the equipment layout, container positions, and materials in diagrams to make them easier to understand.

Chapter 2 defined motion study as a set of techniques for observing and analyzing the actual motions that make up work operations. Another way of looking at motion study is to consider it as one of the current-condition analysis methods for studying and improving operation methods.

## Find the Main Problems

Look again at the issue of problem consciousness that was raised briefly in Chapter 2. Being problem-conscious means looking at the current conditions as they are and asking, Why are we doing it this way? As mentioned earlier, the point of current-condition analysis is to understand conditions as they really are. But you also need to understand which problems are the most important ones. To do that, use the Big 3 problem checklist from Table 3-1. Then follow that up by asking Why? about all the items pointed out on the checklist.

When a problem arises even before the current-condition analysis stage, first find out which of the PQCDSM factors (i.e., productivity, quality, cost, delivery, safety, morale) are most directly related to this problem. Then you will be ready to begin your current-condition analysis. When you have obtained the results of this analysis, use the PQCDSM factors again to help determine what the root problems are and gain a more precise focus for setting improvement goals.

## Draft and Select an Improvement Plan

At the current-condition analysis stage, you merely observed the conditions without taking action. At the improvement planning stage, it is time to look at which problems are most important and to completely change or eliminate the conditions that gave rise to those problems. In other words, your questioning attitude must become more assertive as you ask, Why must things be done that way? and What would happen if we quit doing them that way? Armed with this inquisitive attitude, apply the four improvement principles (eliminate, combine, rearrange, and simplify) while drafting improvement plans.

A good improvement plan is one that makes the operations

- easier (less tiring)
- better (higher quality)
- faster (less time required)
- cheaper (lower costs)

You can achieve all four advantages by drafting improvement plans that eliminate the Big 3 problems. Good improvement plans that arise from such planning efforts usually fall into one of three categories.

1. Quick-fix improvement. This type of plan improves the status quo by making just a small improvement.
2. Some preparation, but good results. This kind of plan requires some minor expenses.

3. Lots of preparation and expenses. This kind of plan is time-consuming and expensive but can be worthwhile from a long-term perspective.

Often, your improvement plan proposals will cover more than one category, in which case you need to decide which plan is most appropriate for the particular improvement goal.

### Carry out the Improvement Plan

Once you have determined which improvement plan proposal is most appropriate at this point, you are ready to think about how the plan should be carried out. If we can confirm the plan's feasibility and gain the necessary approval from higher-ups, we can begin implementing it. After we have implemented the plan and have measured the results, we still need to take periodic follow-up measures. This means fulfilling the CA (check-action) part of the PDCA cycle by checking for further problems and responding with further improvements.

### Keep the PDCA Cycle Turning

This chapter has explained the various parts of the PDCA management cycle, from analyzing current conditions (i.e., motions) to discovering the Big 3 problems, planning an improvement to eliminate them, and checking up on the improvement. Table 3-5 sums up the discussion of improvement steps and the PDCA cycle.

The foundation on which to build your improvement plans is your analysis of current conditions (motions). The final chapters will turn to specific techniques for studying motions, such as therblig analysis. Before getting into that, however, review the principles covered in this chapter through the following case study.

**Table 3-5. Improvement Steps (Summary)**

| Improvement steps (turning the PDCA cycle) |
| --- |

1. The Big 3 problems exist in every workplace (always look critically at the workplace to discover small problems before they become big problems).

   (Use the PQCDSM factors to assist a general check of current conditions.)

2. Carefully study the motions comprising the operations (current-condition analysis).
   - Observe the current motions as they are.
   - Observe the current motions objectively.
   - Observe the current motions quantitatively.
   - Whenever possible, use symbols and graphs to indicate current motions.
   - Use the 5W1H checklist.

3. Discover where the Big 3 problems exist (find the main problems).
   - Be problem-conscious (ask why things are done the current way).
   - Check the current motions against the Big 3 checklist (Table 3-1).
   - Use the PQCDSM factors to prioritize based on the results of the current-condition analysis.

4. Eliminate the Big 3 problems (draft improvement plans).
   - Figure out how the current motions can be improved (apply the four improvement principles).
   - Draft an improvement plan that will make the operations easier (less tiring), better (higher quality), faster (less time required), and cheaper (lower costs).
   - List the improvement points.
   - Meet with others to study the improvement points and assign tasks for implementing the improvement plan.

5. Select a final improvement plan and implement it.

6. After implementing the plan, evaluate it and follow up with further checks and countermeasures (the CA in PDCA).

   Once the improvement is established and stable, standardize it (revise the operation manuals, etc.).

## Improvement Example: Improvement of Roll Shop Operations

You have just seen how the key stages of the PDCA cycle relate to the steps in motion improvements. Now look at a concrete example of motion improvement in a steel company's roll shop operations.

The rollers that are used for rolling steel wear down over time and must be refinished periodically. Two chocks (a type of spindle bearing) extend from the roller necks (see Figure 3-4). The chocks are taken off when the roller needs refinishing, and are put back on again after the roller is refinished.

At this steel company, the roller refinishing operation is simply termed "roll shop operations." This improvement case study will focus on the roller/chock reassembly part of the operations. As Figure 3-4 shows, two rollers have been set up: a working roller and a backup roller. Only the working roller touches the steel plates that are being rolled. The backup roller is still involved in the rolling function, though, because the working roller presses against it when it comes under the pressure of the steel plates that are being rolled. This improvement example concerns the working roller.

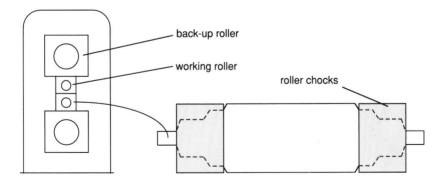

**Figure 3-4. Roller Assembly Operations**

### Step 1: Discover the Problem

At company A, the roll shop was asked to participate in a companywide cost reduction campaign. They began by doing a PQCDSM check to look for problems in the shop operations. Here are the results of that check.

P (Productivity): Has there been a drop in output from roll refinishing and reassembly operations? No.

Q (Quality): Is the roller putting too much pressure on the steel plate? No.

C (Cost): Have grinder costs risen because of increased grinder wear? No. Is there an excess of staffing? Yes.

D (Delivery): Have delays in refinishing and assembly operations caused delivery problems for the roll shop? No.

S (Safety): Do the refinishing and assembly operations include any unsafe operations? No.

M (Morale): Are there any morale problems among the workers? No.

The only problem revealed by this PQCDSM check was that the roll shop's assembly operations had excess staffing relative to other companies' roll shops. The improvement team carried out a preliminary study of current conditions regarding this staffing issue and determined that the issue warranted a full-scale current-condition analysis.

### Step 2: Analyze Current Conditions

So far, the improvement team had conducted a PQCDSM check and had found that the operations seemed to be using more workers than they needed. They next began observing the assembly operations with a critical eye, and came up with the descriptive data shown in Figure 3-5 and Table 3-6.

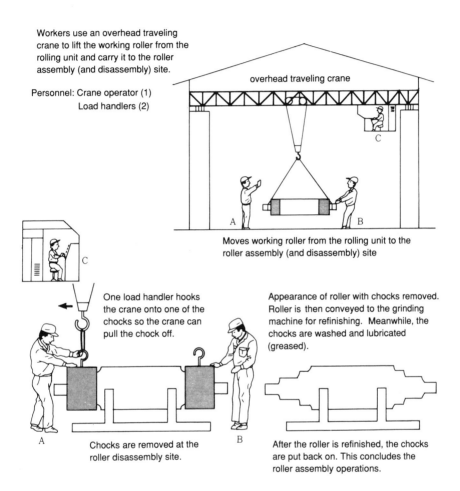

Workers use an overhead traveling crane to lift the working roller from the rolling unit and carry it to the roller assembly (and disassembly) site.

Personnel: Crane operator (1)
Load handlers (2)

overhead traveling crane

Moves working roller from the rolling unit to the roller assembly (and disassembly) site

One load handler hooks the crane onto one of the chocks so the crane can pull the chock off.

Appearance of roller with chocks removed. Roller is then conveyed to the grinding machine for refinishing. Meanwhile, the chocks are washed and lubricated (greased).

Chocks are removed at the roller disassembly site.

After the roller is refinished, the chocks are put back on. This concludes the roller assembly operations.

**Figure 3-5. Description of Current Operations**

Next, the improvement team drew up an operator process chart, shown in Table 3-7 (the method for creating these charts was described in Chapter 2). According to the chart, both worker B and worker C (the crane operator) have a lot of standby time.

**Table 3-6. 5W1H Checklist for Roller Assembly Operations**

| Item | Question | Current condition of operation |
|------|----------|--------------------------------|
| Operator | Who? | Roller assembly workers A and B, crane operator C |
| Time | When? | It takes about one hour to remove, refinish, and reassemble one roller |
| Site | Where? | Roll shop |
| Purpose | Why? | To refinish worn rollers |
| Method | How? | Using an overhead traveling crane (with wire and hook) |
| Target | What? | Removing roller chocks |

### Step 3: Find the Main Problems

At step 2 the improvement team performed the following activities:

1. Operation analysis (observation of operations)
2. Organization of analysis results into 5W1H chart
3. Motion study using operator process analysis for three operators

As suggested by their general (PQCDSM) check back at step 1, the main problem was a cost problem. At step 2, it became clear that two of the workers had a lot of standby time, which means excessive labor costs. Now that they had narrowed their focus down to the main problem, they were ready to dig more deeply by asking Why? about each of the 5W1H factors, as shown in Table 3-8.

### Step 4: Draft and Select an Improvement Plan

When analyzing current conditions, the important thing is to observe and study the facts as they are. After all, you cannot

## Table 3-7.  Operator Process Chart (Three Operators)

| | Worker C (Crane Operator) | | Worker A | | Worker B | |
|---|---|---|---|---|---|---|
| | Step | Flow | Step | Flow | Step | Flow |
| 1 | Move crane from roller assembly site to rolling unit | ○ | Walk from roller assembly site to rolling unit | ○ | Walk from roller assembly site to rolling unit | ○ |
| 2 | Lower wire and hook | ○ | Give guide signals to crane operator | ○ | Stand by | ▽ |
| 3 | Wait for Workers A and B to hook roller onto crane hook | ▽ | Attach wire to left end of roller | ○ | Attach wire to right end of roller | ○ |
| 4 | Raise roller | ○ | Give guide signals to crane operator | ○ | Stand by | ▽ |
| 5 | Begin moving roller to roller disassembly site | ○ | Give guide signals to crane operator | ○ | Stand by | ▽ |
| 6 | Continue moving roller to roller disassembly site | ○ | Walk with roller | ○ | Walk with roller (100 meters) | ○ |
| 7 | Lower roller onto dis-assembly site | ○ | Give guide signals to crane operator | ○ | Stand by | ▽ |
| 8 | Stand by | ▽ | Insert chock removal hook in left chock | ○ | Insert chock removal hook in right chock | ○ |
| 9 | Stand by | ▽ | Attach wire to left chock removal hook | ○ | Attach wire to right chock removal hook | ○ |
| 10 | Remove left chock | ○ | Give guide signals to crane operator | ○ | Stand by | ▽ |
| 11 | Stand by | ▽ | Standby | ▽ | Attach wire to hook | ○ |
| 12 | Remove right chock | ○ | Give guide signals to crane operator | ○ | Assist right chock removal | ○ |
| | Total | ○ ▽ 8 4 | | ○ ○ ▽ 9 2 1 | | ○ ○ ▽ 5 2 5 |

**Table 3-8. Asking "Why?" About the 5W1H Factors**

| 5W1H Factor | Description of Current Condition | Why? | Doubts |
|---|---|---|---|
| Who | Roller assembly workers A and B and crane operator C | Why? | Does it really take three workers to run this operation? |
| When | It takes about one hour to remove, refinish, and reassemble one roller. | Why? | Must it take an hour to perform this job? |
| Where | Roll shop | Why? | Must this job be done at the roll shop? |
| Why | To refinish worn rollers | Why? | Is it necessary to refinish the rollers? |
| How | Using an overhead traveling crane (with hook and wire) | Why? | Must a crane be used to do this job? |
| What | Removing chocks from rollers | Why? | Must the chocks be removed from the rollers? |

learn what needs improving unless you know what is going on in the first place. That is why the improvement team avoided being critical at the current-condition analysis stage and instead just observed the operations and reported the facts objectively.

At the next step, when they questioned the 5W1H factors recorded during the current-condition analysis, they began to think critically. Finally, when they reached step 4 — drafting an improvement plan — they kept thinking critically and applied the four principles for making improvements. Table 3-9 shows how they applied these principles.

Their application of the four improvement principles revealed two main improvement points.

1. The roller refinishing process is necessary, but the roller disassembly/reassembly process can be eliminated (see

## Table 3-9. Application of the Four Improvement Principles

| | Principle | Suggestion | | Check Result |
|---|---|---|---|---|
| 1 | Eliminate | 1. Can the roller refinishing process be eliminated? | No | Since rollers wear down, refinishing is necessary to maintain quality. |
| | | 2. Can the roller disassembly/ reassembly process be eliminated? | Yes | Chocks must be washed, but they can be left on rollers while rollers are refinished. |
| | | 3. Can the overhead traveling crane be eliminated as the transport device for the rollers? | No | Rollers must be moved before being refinished. |
| 2 | Combine | 1. Can the roller refinishing and roller assembly operations be combined? | Yes | Using approach under elimination item 2 above, it is possible to combine them. |
| | | 2. Can the crane operation and load handling tasks be combined? | Yes | Possible if one load handler uses a wireless remote control device to operate the crane. Efficiency may drop at first, however. |
| 3 | Rearrange | 1. Can the roller be refinished without being disassembled? | Yes | Same approach as in elimination item 2 and combination item 1. |
| | | 2. Can the roller be disassembled before being conveyed? | No | This would mean removing roller from rolling unit, then removing chocks before conveying roller to the grinding machine. Workshop layout prohibits this; not a great improvement at any rate. |
| 4 | Simplify | 1. Can the roller refinishing process be simplified? | No | Current refinishing process is most suitable one now available. |
| | | 2. Can the roller disassembly/ reassembly operation be simplified? | Yes | Eliminating roller disassembly/ reassembly operation is the ultimate simplification. This means taking the approach suggested in elimination item 2 and combination item 1. |
| | | 3. Can the roller transport process be simplified? | No | Layout prohibits shortening transport distance. It would be too difficult and costly to change layout for shorter transport. |

Figure 3-6). The chocks can be left on the roller while the roller is being refinished. Occasionally, the chocks will need to be cleaned, however.

2. The roller transport operation's three-person work force can be reduced to two, and perhaps even just one worker (see Figure 3-7). If one of the load handling workers uses a wireless remote control device to operate the overhead traveling crane, they can eliminate the need for a separate crane operator. Further efficiency improvements may even make it possible for the operation to be done by just one worker.

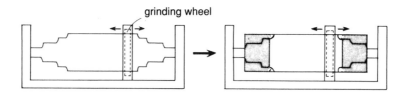

**Figure 3-6. Roller Refinishing Process**

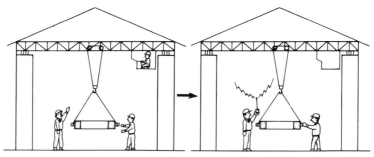

**Figure 3-7. Roller Transport Operation**

Asking themselves what the full implications of these two improvements might be, the improvement team made the following determinations:

1. Refinishing the rollers with the chocks attached will require some major (costly) remodeling of the roller grinding machine. However, the cost savings realized by reducing the staffing requirement is greater than the cost of remodeling the roller grinding machine.

2. Using a wireless remote control device to operate the overhead traveling crane would produce a small cost savings in eliminating the need for a crane operator and is also advisable now that such devices have become inexpensive and very easy to operate.

### Step 5: Implement and Evaluate the Improvement Plan

In this case, two improvement plans were proposed, and the improvement team selected which to implement first on the basis of practical considerations. They then began the improvement planning stage (request for equipment, cost estimate, contract, construction, test run, and operation).

### Step 6: Follow Up on Improvement

The improvement team followed up on their two improvements by making periodic checks and by revising standards and operation manuals to prevent backsliding.

## SUMMARY

This chapter focused on the need for problem consciousness and a clear understanding of current conditions in the workplace. These two things form the foundation for all

## Table 3-10. PDCA Cycle Checkpoints

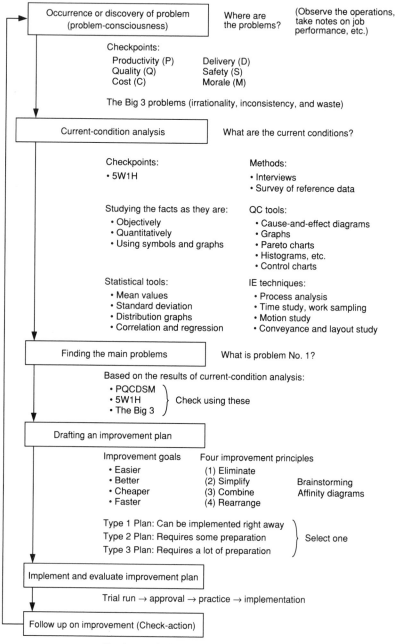

**Occurrence or discovery of problem (problem-consciousness)**

Where are the problems? (Observe the operations, take notes on job performance, etc.)

Checkpoints:
Productivity (P)    Delivery (D)
Quality (Q)    Safety (S)
Cost (C)    Morale (M)

The Big 3 problems (irrationality, inconsistency, and waste)

**Current-condition analysis**

What are the current conditions?

Checkpoints:    Methods:
• 5W1H    • Interviews
    • Survey of reference data

Studying the facts as they are:    QC tools:
• Objectively    • Cause-and-effect diagrams
• Quantitatively    • Graphs
• Using symbols and graphs    • Pareto charts
    • Histograms, etc.
    • Control charts

Statistical tools:    IE techniques:
• Mean values    • Process analysis
• Standard deviation    • Time study, work sampling
• Distribution graphs    • Motion study
• Correlation and regression    • Conveyance and layout study

**Finding the main problems**

What is problem No. 1?

Based on the results of current-condition analysis:
• PQCDSM
• 5W1H    } Check using these
• The Big 3

**Drafting an improvement plan**

Improvement goals    Four improvement principles
• Easier    (1) Eliminate
• Better    (2) Simplify    Brainstorming
• Cheaper    (3) Combine    Affinity diagrams
• Faster    (4) Rearrange

Type 1 Plan: Can be implemented right away
Type 2 Plan: Requires some preparation    } Select one
Type 3 Plan: Requires a lot of preparation

**Implement and evaluate improvement plan**

Trial run → approval → practice → implementation

**Follow up on improvement (Check-action)**

Check up on the improvement after it is established and promptly make further improvements to correct any problems that are discovered.

improvements. When it comes to making improvements, every-thing depends on how well you understand the conditions to be improved.

Table 3-10 lists the checkpoints at each stage in the PDCA cycle and summarizes the methods discussed in this chapter. This table should help the reader understand where motion study fits into the overall scheme of improvement techniques.

# 4

# Introduction to Therblig Analysis

Therblig analysis was briefly described in Chapter 2 as one of the four types of motion study. After using operator process analysis to get an overall understanding of the process, you might use therblig analysis to take a more detailed look at the process. This chapter introduces therblig analysis in more detail, and Chapter 5 will describe how to use this analysis for making process improvements.

## WHAT IS A THERBLIG?

Figure 3-3 in Chapter 3 showed how current condition analysis fits into the overall management (PDCA) cycle as one step in the cycle. Motion study is one of the methods you can use to carry out the current-condition analysis step. Therblig analysis, in turn, is a type of motion study.

Chapter 3 also listed the four main requirements of current-condition analysis:

- Study the facts as they are
- Be objective

- Express the facts in quantitative terms
- Use symbols and charts

Developed by Frank Gilbreth, therblig analysis uses 18 categories and graphic symbols (each called a therblig) to indicate specific "fundamental motions."* As such, therbligs offer the following advantages:

1. They help you describe the facts as they are.
2. They help you analyze current conditions objectively.
3. The symbols or their letter equivalents are easier to recognize and organize than lengthy textual descriptions.

## THE THERBLIG ANALYSIS METHOD

### Terms and Symbols Used in Therblig Analysis

Each therblig indicates a particular hand, arm, or eye motion. The therblig symbols can be combined to express motions used in all kinds of operations. This section describes the fundamental motions that correspond to each therblig (see Table 4-1).

The therbligs are divided into three types of motions:

Type 1: Motions required for performing an operation
Type 2: Motions that tend to slow down the first type of motion
Type 3: Motions that do not perform an operation

---

* In Japan, the pictographic therblig symbols are widely known and used for motion study, and the charts prepared for this book employ them extensively. As some Western authorities feel that these symbols are difficult to learn, the letter symbols have been included in the descriptions of each therblig and in key reference figures within Chapters 4 and 5. These letters can be used interchangeably with the pictographic symbols according to the user's preference. — Ed.

## Table 4-1. Therblig Symbols (18 motions)

| Type | Name of Motion | Letters/ Symbol | Description or Pictographic Meaning |
|---|---|---|---|
| Type 1: Motions required for performing an operation | 1. Transport empty | ⌣ TE | Empty palm |
| | 2. Grasp | ∩ G | Hand open for grasping |
| | 3. Transport loaded (carry) | ᴗ TL | Hand carrying something |
| | 4. Position | ⌾ P | Object being placed by hand |
| | 5. Disassemble | ⊷ DA | Part of assembly removed |
| | 6. Use | U U | Letter "U" from the word "Use" |
| | 7. Assemble | ♯ A | Several things put together |
| | 8. Release load | ⌒ RL | Dropping content from hand |
| | 9. Inspect | ◊ I | Shape of a magnifying lens |
| Type 2: Motions that tend to slow down Type 1 motion | 10. Search | ⊂⊃ Sh | Eye turned to look |
| | 11. Find | ⊙ F | Eye finding object |
| | 12. Select | → St | Pointing to object |
| | 13. Plan | ⌘ Pn | Person thinking |
| | 14. Pre-position (setup) | ⌗ PP | Bowling pin ("set up") |
| Type 3: Motions that do not perform an operation | 15. Hold | ⌂ H | Magnet holding a bar |
| | 16. Unavoidable delay | ⌒ UD | Person falling accidentally |
| | 17. Avoidable delay (standby) | ⌣ AD | Person lying down voluntarily |
| | 18. Rest | ⌐ R | Person seated |

To make it easier to understand the therblig definitions, the following examples, based on simple activities such as writing a letter with a fountain pen, are given.

## Type 1 Motions

Type 1 motion is any motion that picks up, uses, processes, combines, or otherwise manipulates an object that is essential to the operation (such as a part, material, jig, tool, and so on). Type 1 also includes motions involved in straightening up after an operation. Put simply, the type 1 motion is any motion that is required for performing an operation. Therbligs 1 through 9 fall into the type 1 category.

### 1. Transport Empty ( ⌣ or TE)

*Transport empty* indicates a hand that is moving while empty. It could be moving for a specific purpose or it could be moving back after having moved for a specific purpose. In the first case, this motion will inevitably be followed by a *grasp* motion and in the second case, the hand is simply returning to its previous position.

Figure 4-1 illustrates a situation in which the operation begins and ends with a transport empty motion. As Table 4-2 shows, the first transport empty is for a specific purpose, namely, to select a fountain pen from the pens and pencils on the table. The last one is to move the hand back after moving it for a specific purpose, which in this case was to return the fountain pen to its original position.

### 2. Grasp ( ⌒ or G)

Here, the hand touching the object is what completes the previous transport empty motion. Next, the hand grasps the object. This motion ends when the hand begins to carry the object

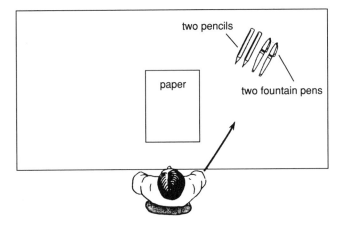

**Figure 4-1. Writing a Letter with a Fountain Pen**

**Table 4-2. Transport Empty**

| Left hand motion | Therblig | | Right hand motion |
| --- | --- | --- | --- |
| | Left hand | Right hand | |
| | | ⌣ | Reach for fountain pen. |
| | | ⌣ | Return hand to original position. |

somewhere. Table 4-3 shows how this second motion follows the first, based on the diagram shown in Figure 4-1.

### 3. Transport Loaded ( ⌣ or TL)

Basically, *transport loaded* (also called *carry*) occurs when a hand that is holding something moves (carries the object) from

**Table 4-3. Grasp**

| Left hand motion | Therblig | | Right hand motion |
|---|---|---|---|
| | Left hand | Right hand | |
| | | ◡ | Reach for fountain pen. |
| | | ∩ | Grasp pen. |
| | | | ⋮ |

one place to another. The hand may be doing this in any number of ways, such as

- carrying through the air
- pushing
- sliding
- pulling
- dragging
- rolling

The transport loaded motion begins when the loaded object starts to move and ends when the object stops moving. A grasp motion always precedes a transport loaded motion. Table 4-4 shows this in the form of grasping a fountain pen and carrying it to the letter paper.

#### *4. Position (୨ or P)*

The *position* motion puts the object in the correct position for the next motion, moving it while or after it is carried. People do this motion quite often in their everyday activities. Figure 4-2 shows the position motion used in preparing to get a glass of water from a bottle. As the figure implies, the right hand

**Table 4-4. Transport Loaded**

| Left hand motion | Therblig | | Right hand motion |
| --- | --- | --- | --- |
| | Left hand | Right hand | |
| | | ∪ | Reach for fountain pen. |
| | | ∩ | Grasp pen. |
| | | ◡ | Carry pen to paper. |

1. reaches toward the glass (TE)
2. grasps the glass (G)
3. lifts and turns over the glass (TL + P)
4. puts down the glass

**Figure 4-2. Glass and Bottle**

In this case, the hand positions the glass (turns it right-side up to hold water) while transporting it. After the drink is taken, the transport loaded motion must again be combined with a position motion to turn the cup upside down again before placing it on top of the bottle.

A similar combination of motions occurs in the operation illustrated in Figure 4-1. These motions are listed separately in Table 4-5.

**Table 4-5. Position**

| Left hand motion | Therblig | | Right hand motion |
| | Left hand | Right hand | |
|---|---|---|---|
| | | ⌣ | Reach for fountain pen. |
| | | ∩ | Grasp pen. |
| | | ᓆ | Turn pen to writing position. |
| | | ⌡ | Carry pen to paper. |

To indicate this combination of positioning and transporting a load, you can combine the therbligs with a plus sign (ᴗ + ᓆ or TL + P); see Table 4-6.

**Table 4-6. Position/Transport Loaded**

| Left hand motion | Therblig | | Right hand motion |
| | Left hand | Right hand | |
|---|---|---|---|
| | | ⌣ | Reach for fountain pen. |
| | | ∩ | Grasp pen. |
| | | ᴗ+ᓆ | Turn pen to writing position while carrying pen to paper. |

## 5. Disassemble ( ++ or DA)

*Disassemble* is the motion of taking apart something that has been put together. For simplicity's sake, the fountain pen example has so far excluded any reference to a cap on the pen.

Since most fountain pens do have caps, the example will next apply this motion to removal of the cap for use.

In this operation, the right hand first reaches for the fountain pen, grasps it, and carries it while positioning it so that the left hand can easily reach the cap.

At first, the left hand does not do anything. As soon as the right hand has finished carrying and positioning the pen, the left hand reaches for the cap. Next, the left hand grasps the cap and then removes (disassembles) it. While the left hand is removing the cap, the right hand is pulling at the pen. Table 4-7 shows a therblig analysis chart describing this series of motions.

**Table 4-7. Disassemble**

| Left hand motion | Therblig | | Right hand motion |
| --- | --- | --- | --- |
| | Left hand | Right hand | |
| | | ⌣ | Reach for fountain pen. |
| | | ∩ | Grasp pen. |
| | | ⌣+⦶ | Turn pen to writing position while carrying pen to paper. |
| Reach for cap on pen. | ⌣ | | |
| Grasp cap on pen. | ∩ | | |
| Remove cap from pen. | ++ | ++ | Pull pen. |

## 6. Use ( ∪ or U)

The *use* motion is any motion that uses the object for a particular purpose. In the fountain pen example, after removing the cap from the fountain pen, the left hand will carry the cap to the table top. Meanwhile, the right hand carries out a series of motions that includes "carry uncapped pen to paper while positioning it for writing" and "use pen to write" (i.e., write the text of the letter).

Table 4-8 shows a therblig analysis chart describing this series of motions.

**Table 4-8.  Use**

| Left hand motion | Therblig | | Right hand motion |
|---|---|---|---|
| | **Left hand** | **Right hand** | |
| | | ⌣ | Reach for fountain pen. |
| | | ∩ | Grasp pen. |
| | | ⌣+◑ | Turn pen cap toward left hand while carrying pen toward left hand. |
| Reach for cap on pen. | ⌣ | | |
| Grasp cap on pen. | ∩ | | |
| Remove cap from pen. | ⊦⊦ | ⊦⊦ | Pull pen. |
| Carry cap to table top. | ⌣+◑ | ⌣+◑ | Turn pen to writing position while carrying pen to paper. |
| | | ∪ | Write letter. |

## 7. Assemble ( ⊞ or A)

The *assemble* motion is any motion that inserts or adds one object into or onto another object. Virtually no assemble motions work well unless they are preceded by a position motion.

In the fountain pen example, the string of motions that the left hand begins once the writer has finished writing the letter consists of "reach for cap on table top," "grasp cap," "position cap hole toward pen held in right hand while moving cap to pen," and "put cap back (i.e., assemble cap) onto the fountain pen."

Meanwhile, the right hand's sequence of motions are "lift pen from paper," position tip of pen toward cap in left hand while moving pen toward cap," and "insert (i.e., assemble) pen tip into cap." Table 4-9 shows a therblig analysis chart describing this series of motions.

### 8. Release Load ( ⌒ or RL)

The *release load* motion is any motion that lets go of an object; usually it is a motion that is performed when the operator has finished using or transporting the object.

In the fountain pen example, release load is the third motion in the series described in section 5 above, namely, "remove cap," "carry cap to table top," and "put cap down (i.e., release the cap) onto table top." Table 4-10 shows a therblig analysis chart of how this release motion is added onto the other motions already listed in Table 4-9.

### 9. Inspect ( () or I)

The *inspect* motion generally involves checking finished goods against the relevant quantity and quality standards. As such, the actual act of inspecting is a basically mental type of motion that lasts only a few seconds and is often done in parallel with other motions.

In the letter-writing example, the inspect motion involves checking each word as it is written to look for errors. This motion is shown in Table 4-11.

**Table 4-9. Assemble**

| Left hand motion | Therblig | | Right hand motion |
|---|---|---|---|
| | **Left hand** | **Right hand** | |
| | | ∪ | Reach for fountain pen. |
| | | ∩ | Grasp pen. |
| | | ↺+⊃ | Turn pen cap toward left hand while carrying pen toward left hand. |
| Reach for cap on pen. | ∪ | | |
| Grasp cap on pen. | ∩ | | |
| Remove cap from pen. | ++ | ++ | Pull pen. |
| Carry cap to table top. | ↺+⊃ | ↺+⊃ | Turn pen to writing position while carrying pen to paper. |
| | | ∪ | Write letter. |
| Reach for cap on table top. | ∪ | | |
| Grasp cap. | ∩ | | |
| Position cap hole toward pen held in right hand while moving cap to pen. | ↺+⊃ | ↺+⊃ | Lift pen from paper and position tip of pen toward cap in left hand while moving pen toward cap. |
| Put cap back (i.e., assemble the cap) onto the pen. | ⊞ | ⊞ | Insert (assemble) pen tip into cap. |

## Table 4-10. Release

| Left hand motion | Therblig | | Right hand motion |
| --- | --- | --- | --- |
| | Left hand | Right hand | |
| | | ⌣ | Reach for fountain pen. |
| | | ∩ | Grasp pen. |
| | | ↜+⌣ | Turn pen cap toward left hand while carrying pen toward left hand. |
| Reach for cap on pen. | ⌣ | | |
| Grasp cap on pen. | ∩ | | |
| Remove cap from pen. | ++ | ++ | Pull pen. |
| Carry cap to table top. | ↜+⌣ | | |
| Release cap on table top. | ⌒ | ↜+⌣ | Carry pen to letter paper. |
| | | U | Write letter. |
| | | ↜ | Lift pen from paper. |
| Reach for cap on table top. | ⌣ | | |
| Grasp cap. | ∩ | | |
| Position cap hole toward pen held in right hand while moving cap to pen. | ↜+⌣ | ↜+⌣ | Carry pen toward cap. |
| Put the cap back onto the pen. | ♯ | ♯ | Insert (assemble) pen tip into cap. |

**Table 4-11. Inspect**

| Left hand motion | Therblig | | Right hand motion |
|---|---|---|---|
| | Left hand | Right hand | |
| | | U + 0 | Inspect words while writing letter. |

## Type 2 Motions

To find out whether parts, materials, and tools are in good order, you must examine their conditions. This kind of activity requires more thinking than doing. Such motions can be grouped together as type 2 motions — those that tend to slow down the type 1 motion. Therbligs 10 through 14 fall into this category.

### 10. Search (◯ or Sh)

When we use the word "search" in everyday conversation, we are almost always talking about something we do with our eyes. In motion study, however, searching is also something done with the nose (searching for odors), the ears (searching for noises), and other sensory organs. However, this broad meaning is not conveyed by the therblig symbol for searching, which is a pictograph of an eye looking sideways.

In defining the motions, *search* is used to indicate the motion that starts when a person begins to search and ends just before he or she finds the object of the search. Sometimes the start and stop of the search is a fairly subjective determination. Three guidelines offer some assistance:

- It is not a search if you already know what the object is and know approximately where it is, but are merely deciding how to position it.
- On the other hand, consider it searching if you already know what the object is but do not know where it is — as might be the case when it is hidden from view by something.
- Naturally, this searching motion comes to an end as soon as you pick up or otherwise remove the thing that blocks the view of the object.

Refer again to the fountain pen example in Figure 4-1. Since the fountain pen is lying with some pencils on the desk, before the writer can grasp the pen there will be a brief moment in which he or she searches for it among the group of writing utensils. Since this search motion is an eye motion rather than a left- or right-hand motion, a column for eye movements is included in the therblig analysis chart (see Table 4-12).

**Table 4-12. Search**

| Left hand motion | Therblig | | | Right hand motion |
|---|---|---|---|---|
| | Left hand | Eyes | Right hand | |
| | | ⟳ | | Search for fountain pen. |
| | | | ⌣ | Reach for pen. |

### 11. Find ( ⬭ or F)

The *find* motion occurs on the heels of the search motion to mark the finding of whatever object the person has been searching for. Like search, find usually lasts only a few seconds. Table 4-13 shows the therblig analysis chart for this motion in the fountain pen example.

**Table 4-13. Find**

| Left hand motion | Therblig | | | Right hand motion |
|---|---|---|---|---|
| | Left hand | Eyes | Right hand | |
| | | ⬭ | | Search for fountain pen. |
| | | ⬭ | | Find fountain pen amid other writing utensils. |
| | | | ⌣ | Reach for fountain pen. |

### 12. Select ( → or St)

The *select* motion usually follows searching for an object and finding a group that contains the object. It indicates selecting the object from the group. In the fountain pen example, the writer has searched for a fountain pen and has found two among a group of writing utensils. The writer then selects one pen (see Table 4-14).

All three of the type 2 motions just described — searching, finding, and selecting — occur during the overall process of reaching for (or going to pick up) an object. Consequently, these eye motions are usually done in parallel with a hand motion, such as a reaching motion (transport empty). On a therblig analysis chart, the notations for search and find are usually entered before the notation for the parallel transport empty hand motion.

**Table 4-14. Select**

| Left hand motion | Therblig | | | Right hand motion |
|---|---|---|---|---|
| | Left hand | Eyes | Right hand | |
| | | ○ | | Search for fountain pen. |
| | | ⊙ | | Find pen amid other writing utensils. |
| | | → | | Select one pen from the two. |
| | | | ∪ | Reach for pen. |
| | | | ⋮ | ⋮ |

### *13. Plan ( ℓ or Pn)*

*Plan* is a mental activity that occurs, for example, when you must decide on or analyze something. There is no corresponding eye motion. Planning can occur before, during, or after physical motions. Referring again to the letter-writing example, you can add planning to the other writing motions to emphasize the thinking that goes into writing (see Table 4-15).

**Table 4-15. Plan**

| Left hand motion | Therblig | | | Right hand motion |
|---|---|---|---|---|
| | Left hand | Eyes | Right hand | |
| | | | ⋮ | |
| | | | U+ℓ | Write letter while thinking. |
| | | | ⋮ | |

### 14. Pre-position (8 or PP)

The *pre-position* (setup) motion is often used during repetitive operations. It involves positioning an object beforehand so that it will not have to be positioned while being conveyed or used. For example, after picking up a teapot by its handle, pouring out a cup of tea, and putting the teapot back, you might pre-position the handle upright so that it is easier for the next person to reach.

## Type 3 Motion

The type 3 motion consists of activities that prevent an operation from happening and result in a delay or a standby in which the operator must merely hold an object for the time being. Therbligs 15 through 18 are type 3 motions — those that do not contribute to an operation.

### 15. Hold ( ⌂ or H)

The *hold* "motion" indicates that the object is just being held and is not being used for anything. This can be a situation in which the object is held after the operator has reached for and grasped it, or in which the object is held after the operator has also carried it somewhere.

Refer back to Table 4-10, which describes the fountain pen example. There you can see some blank space in the "right-hand motion" column under the motion described as "turn pen cap toward left hand while carrying pen toward left hand." However, the right hand is still doing something between this motion and the end of the next one in the table ("remove cap from pen"). It is holding the pen. Later, the right hand has a very brief holding motion while the writer reaches with the left hand toward the cap on the table top.

If you keep looking closer at the letter-writing operation, you will also notice that the left hand is busy holding the paper

**Table 4-16. Hold**

| Left hand motion | Therblig | | | Right hand motion |
| --- | --- | --- | --- | --- |
| | Left hand | Eyes | Right hand | |
| | | ⌒ ⌒→ | | Search for fountain pen. Select fountain pen. |
| | | | ⌣ | Reach for pen. |
| | | | ∩ | Grasp pen. |
| | | | ᴗ+૭ | Turn pen cap toward left hand while carrying pen toward left hand. |
| Reach for cap on pen. | ⌣ | | ⌂ | Hold pen. |
| Grasp cap on pen. | ∩ | | ⌂ | Hold pen. |
| Remove cap from pen. | ⟷ | | ⟷ | Pull pen. |
| Carry cap to table top. | ᴗ+૭ | | ⌂ | Hold pen. |
| Release cap on table top. | ⌒ | | ⌂ | Hold pen. |
| Reach for bottom edge of paper. | ⌣ | | ⌂ | Hold pen. |
| Grasp paper. | ∩ | | ᴗ+૭ | Carry pen to paper while correcting its position. |
| Hold letter paper. | ⌂ | | U+૪ | Use pen to write letter. |
| Release hand from paper. | ⌒ | | ⌒ | Lift pen from paper. |
| Reach for cap on table top. | ⌣ | | ⌂ | Hold pen. |
| Grasp cap. | ∩ | | ⌂ | Hold pen. |
| Position cap hole toward pen held in right hand while moving cap to pen. | ᴗ+૭ | | ᴗ+૭ | Carry pen toward cap. |
| Put cap back onto pen. | ⌗ | | ⌗ | Insert (assemble) pen tip into cap. |

in place while the right hand is writing. This holding motion is preceded by two other left-hand motions after the left hand releases the pen cap on the table top — "reach for bottom edge of paper" and "grasp paper." Table 4-16 shows how the contents of Table 4-10 can be expanded to more fully describe the motions involved in the letter-writing example.

### 16. Unavoidable delay (⌒ or UD)

*Unavoidable delay* indicates a delay caused by something for which the operator is not responsible. For example, the operator may have an object prepared to be transported, but if the crane or truck that is supposed to do the conveying has not arrived, an unavoidable delay occurs.

### 17. Avoidable Delay (⌣ or AD)

An *avoidable delay* is a delay or standby that can be eliminated if the right kind of change or improvement is made. For example, the operator may have only one hand free for doing work because the materials or parts are inconveniently positioned. In such cases, improving the layout of the materials or parts could enable the operator to use both hands. If so, the operator's one-handed work contains an avoidable delay. One of the main points of therblig analysis is to find avoidable delays and to make improvements that eliminate them. The next chapters will present more detailed examples of how this can be done.

### 18. Rest (↵ or R)

*Rest* indicates that the operator is resting, perhaps to recover from fatigue. Naturally, no work is being done at this point.

# 5

# Using Therblig Analysis in Operation Improvement

## STEPS IN THERBLIG ANALYSIS

Chapter 4 used a letter-writing example to explain the 18 fundamental motions and their corresponding therbligs. This chapter will discuss how to use therbligs for current-condition analysis and will outline the most important points to remember during such an analysis.

Of the steps in creating therblig analysis charts, the first step is by far the most important.

*Step 1: Take your time and carefully observe the overall operations.* The person observing the operations should observe them until he or she knows them well enough to picture them in memory.

*Step 2: Sit down and write out the steps in the operation, starting with just one hand's motions (either hand is OK).* Of course, while writing out one hand's motions, you will also be reminded of what the other hand is doing. After completing a basic description of one hand, go on to describe the other hand's motions and how the two hands work together.

*Step 3: After making a basic description, go back with the description and observe the operations again.* Check your description against what you observe in the operations to see if anything was omitted or incorrectly described. Again, it is very important to take all the time you need to come up with an accurate description of the operations.

*Step 4: Sit down again and fill out a therblig analysis form (such as that shown in Table 5-1).* The items to enter on this form include the factory where the operations take place, the name(s) of the operator(s), the observation date, the observer's name, and the layout of the operations (see Table 5-1).

*Step 5: After studying the current-condition analysis performed at step 3, describe the motions in more detail, using the therblig categories.* It will be easier to read the information later on if you also group the detailed motions according to the broader function they are performing. These functions are called work elements. Another hint is to number the work elements as you write them so you can quickly see how many there are. Table 5-2 shows how to do this for the nut-and-bolt assembly example that was introduced in Chapter 2.

*Step 6: Complete the form by adding in the therblig symbols or letters (see Table 5-2).*

## USING THE PRINCIPLES OF MOTION ECONOMY

Once you have completed the therblig analysis, you can use it to find out where the most important problem points are. As Chapter 4 explained, there are three types of motions (and their corresponding therbligs):

1. Motions required for performing an operation
2. Motions that tend to slow down type 1 motions
3. Motions that do not perform an operation

From an improvement perspective, the whole point of doing a therblig analysis is to eliminate type 3 motions while

## Table 5-1. Therblig Analysis Chart Form

Date: _____

| Process (factory): | Operation layout diagram | | | | | |
|---|---|---|---|---|---|---|
| **Product:** | | | | | | |
| **Operators:** | | | | | | |
| **Observer:** | | | | | | |
| **Dept.:** | | | | | | |

| No. | Work element | Left hand motion | Therblig | | | Right hand motion | Comments (positive and improvement-oriented) |
|---|---|---|---|---|---|---|---|
| | | | Left | Eyes | Right | | |
| | | | | | | | |
| | | | | | | | |
| | | | | | | | |
| | | | | | | | |
| | | | | | | | |
| | | | | | | | |

| Summary | Type | Type 1 | | | | | | | | | | Type 2 | | | | | | Type 3 | | | | | Total |
|---|---|---|---|---|---|---|---|---|---|---|---|---|---|---|---|---|---|---|---|---|---|---|---|
| | Therbligs and letters | ∪ TE | ∩ G | ᴜ TL | ꝯ P | ♯ A | ↔ DA | ∪ U | ⌒ RL | ◊ I | No | ⊂ Sh | ⊂⊃ F | → St | ȣ Pn | 8 PP | No | △ H | ⌒ UD | ⌣ AD | ⌐ R | No | |
| | Left hand | | | | | | | | | | | | | | | | | | | | | | |
| | Right hand | | | | | | | | | | | | | | | | | | | | | | |
| | Eyes | | | | | | | | | | | | | | | | | | | | | | |

**Table 5-2. Therblig Analysis of Nut and Bolt Assembly Operation**

| No. | Work element | Left hand motion | Therblig | | | Right hand motion |
|---|---|---|---|---|---|---|
| | | | Left hand | Eyes | Right hand | |
| 1 | Prepare bolt | Reach for bolt. | ⌣ | ⊗ | ∪ᵒ | Stand by. |
| 2 | | Grasp bolt. | ∩ | | ∪ᵒ | Stand by. |
| 3 | | Carry bolt to assembly site. | ⌣+ᵒ | | ∪ᵒ | Stand by. |
| 4 | Prepare nut | Hold bolt. | ⌂ | ⊗ | ⌣ | Reach for nut. |
| 5 | | Hold bolt. | ⌂ | | ∩ | Grasp nut. |
| 6 | | Hold bolt. | ⌂ | | ⌣+ᵒ | Carry nut to assembly site. |
| 7 | Assemble | Assemble nut and bolt. | ♯ | | ♯ | Assemble nut and bolt. |

finding ways to minimize type 2 motions. Naturally, it would be best to eliminate all three types as much as possible. Even when a motion cannot be eliminated, however, there are other ways to make improvements, such as by changing the position of the workpiece to save time.

This section presents some specific checkpoints incorporating the principles of motion economy for you to use in looking for ways to improve the way work is done.* Table 5-3 summarizes these checkpoints, and Table 5-20 (at the end of the chapter) provides a more complete list of checkpoints, arranged in sets related to specific therblig motions.

---

* Checkpoints 4 through 9 are adapted from material found in Ralph M. Barnes, *Motion and Time Study/Design and Measurement of Work* (New York: John Wiley & Sons, 1958) and in Rintaro Muramatsu, *Work Measurement and Case Studies* (Kyoritsu Shuppan, 1958).

**Table 5-3.  Summary of Therblig Analysis Checkpoints (Principles of Motion Economy)**

|  | Checkpoint |
|---|---|
| 1 | Is the operation performed in a way that permits both hands to be working and moving symmetrically in opposite directions? |
| 2 | Does the operation keep required eye movements to a minimum? |
| 3 | Does the operation keep required body movements to a minimum? |
| 4 | Are holding motions kept to a minimum? |
| 5 | Are the parts or materials to be processed or assembled kept where they are easy to pick up? |
| 6 | Are objects positioned so that they can be used as soon as they are grasped? |
| 7 | Does the operation include any unnecessary transportation of assembled or processed items? |
| 8 | Do the work processes that make up the operation flow smoothly, with an easy rhythm? |
| 9 | Even when only one hand is being used, can smooth, continuous, curved motions be used instead of straight motions with sharp changes in direction? |
| 10 | Does the workplace lighting put a strain on the eyes or the work operations? |
| 11 | Are the work table and chair adjusted to the proper height to make the work easiest? |

*Checkpoint 1: Is the operation performed in a way that permits both hands to be working and moving symmetrically in opposite directions?* To understand what it means to move symmetrically in opposite directions, refer again to the nut-and-bolt assembly example, as shown in Figure 5-1. In parts 1 and 2,

the worker must move both hands in the same direction when reaching for a nut and a bolt, but in part 3 she moves them symmetrically, in opposite directions to pick up the two parts.

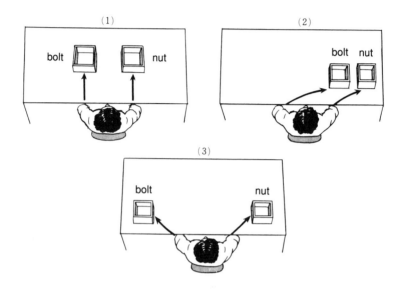

**Figure 5-1. Nut and Bolt Assembly Operation**

If you observe the assembly worker trying to perform the operation using each of these three layouts, you will find that the first two require her to make awkward motions. The third layout, on the other hand, enables her to keep her upper torso balanced and her motions smooth. This means that she will accumulate less stress and fatigue when working.

When work motions are balanced, there is less stress on the mind and body, and the work becomes easier and more enjoyable. Therefore, symmetrical movement is something always to watch for when observing current conditions, and to note when making operation layout diagrams.

Checkpoint 1 also asks whether both hands are kept busy. Referring back to the letter-writing example, look again at the motion described as "remove cap from pen." Figure 5-2 shows the layout of this example and Table 5-4 shows the therblig analysis chart.

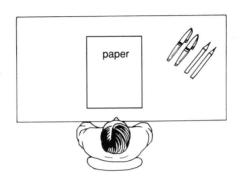

**Figure 5-2. Writing a Letter with a Fountain Pen (1)**

**Table 5-4. Therblig Analysis Chart**

| No. | Work element | Left hand motion | Left hand | Eyes | Right hand | Right hand motion |
|---|---|---|---|---|---|---|
| | | | **Therblig** | | | |
| 1 | Pick up fountain pen | Stand by. | ⌒ʔ | ◯ ⊕ | ⌣ | Search for and select fountain pen while reaching for it. |
| 2 | | Stand by. | ⌒ʔ | | ∩ | Grasp pen. |
| 3 | | Stand by. | ⌒ʔ | | ⌣ + ᶇ | Carry pen toward left hand while adjusting its position. |
| 4 | Remove cap | Reach for cap on pen. | ⌣ | | ⌂ | Hold pen. |
| 5 | | Grasp cap on pen. | ∩ | | ⌂ | Hold pen. |
| 6 | | Remove cap. | ⊦⊦ | | ⊦⊦ | Pull pen. |

As Table 5-4 shows, the left hand's standby status during work elements 1, 2, and 3 is a type 3 motion, namely, avoidable delays. The same category applies to the right hand's motions during work elements 4 and 5. This is a good time to think of checkpoint 1 and ask whether both hands can be kept busy. The rule of thumb here is that it is always more efficient to have both hands working at once than to have one hand work while the other hand is idle or is simply holding something.

To improve the activity, you might consider changing the layout to that shown in Figure 5-3. This layout enables two-handed motion, because having the fountain pen in front of the letter writer enables him to reach with both hands so that he can remove the cap while carrying the pen back to the paper. Table 5-5 shows the therblig analysis chart that describes this set of motions.

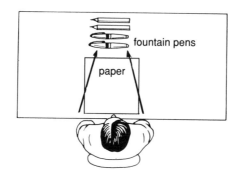

**Figure 5-3. Writing a Letter with a Fountain Pen (2)**

This improvement keeps both hands busy, eliminating three instances of type 3 motion (standby) for the left hand and two instances (holding) for the right hand. The overall effect of the improvement is to reduce the total number of motions from 13 to 8.

The key point to remember here is that both hands should move simultaneously and symmetrically (i.e., in opposite directions). The human body happens to work most easily and

**Table 5-5. Therblig Analysis Chart**

| No. | Work element | Left hand motion | Therblig | | | Right hand motion |
| --- | --- | --- | --- | --- | --- | --- |
| | | | Left hand | Eyes | Right hand | |
| 1 | Pick up fountain pen | Reach for fountain pen. | ∪ | ◯ ⊕ | ∪ | Search for and select fountain pen while reaching for it. |
| 2 | | Grasp pen. | ∩ | | ∩ | Grasp pen. |
| 3 | Remove cap | Remove cap while carrying pen to paper. | ⌣ + ↔ | | ⌣ + ↔ | Pull pen while carrying pen to paper. |

smoothly when the left and right sides are doing similar things. Therefore, stay aware of the need to keep tools and other materials at equal distances from the left and right hands to enable such balanced movement.

Some types of two-handed motions are amenable to simultaneous layout and some are not. Table 5-6 shows the results of a study done on this topic.

In Table 5-6, the intersection of reach on the horizontal and vertical axes has an "A," which means that it should be easy to use both hands at once to reach for something. In the improved letter-writing example (Figure 5-3), there are three simultaneous motions:

1. Both hands reach at once.
2. Both hands grasp at once.
3. Both hands remove cap while carrying pen at once.

According to Table 5-6, the first motion is an "A," and the second and third are "B"s. This means that, with practice, a worker should be able to perform each of these motions using both hands, within the field of vision. The letter grades in this chart make it useful for evaluating improvement proposals.

**Table 5-6. Motions and Simultaneity**

| Left hand \ Right hand | Reach | Move | Turn | Grasp | Position | Dis-assemble | Re-lease | Apply force |
|---|---|---|---|---|---|---|---|---|
| Reach | A | A | A | B | B | B | A | B |
| Move | A | A | A | B | B | B | A | B |
| Turn | A | A | A | B | B | B | A | B |
| Grasp | B | B | B | B | C | C | A | C |
| Position | B | B | B | C | B | C | A | C |
| Disassemble | B | B | B | C | C | A | A | A |
| Release | A | A | A | A | A | A | A | A |
| Apply force | B | B | B | C | C | A | A | A |

Notes
A = Left and right hands can easily move in combination.
B = Hands can move in combination only within the field of vision.
C = Hands generally cannot move simultaneously and should not be required to.

Source: Adapted from H.B. Maynard, G.J. Stegemerten, and J.L. Schwab, *Methods-Time Measurement* (New York: McGraw-Hill, 1948), p. 123.

*Checkpoint 2: Does the operation keep required eye movements to a minimum?* This checkpoint goes beyond the simultaneous hand motions from checkpoint 1 and inquires into something that is a prerequisite for simultaneous, symmetrical hand motions: keeping the hands (and therefore the parts and tools to be handled) within the field of vision.

Unless the objects to be picked up are within the worker's field of vision, he or she must turn the gaze (and perhaps the head and/or torso) toward them to carry out the search, find, and select motions (all type 2 motions). The loss of time incurred by having to turn toward an object may be slight, but it adds up quickly when reaching for objects is a repeated part of the overall operation.

Applying this lesson to the nut-and-bolt assembly example, look at Figure 5-4, a diagram of assembly working conditions that need improvement, and Table 5-7, a therblig analysis chart of these conditions.

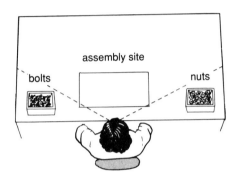

**Figure 5-4. Operation Layout (Before Improvement)**

If you change the operation layout so that both the nut box and the bolt box are within the worker's field of vision, your new layout might look something like Figure 5-5. The new conditions are recorded in the therblig analysis chart shown in Table 5-8.

This example underlines the importance of eliminating all unnecessary eye movements. Many other examples could be given to support this point, such as an assembly operation involving two components and one tool, where an improvement that reduced the number of search sequences (search, find, and select) from three to two per work cycle resulted in a significant cycle time reduction (from 3.5 seconds to just 1.5 seconds).

**Table 5-7. Therblig Analysis Chart (Conditions Before Improvement)**

| No. | Work element | Left hand motion | Therblig | | | Right hand motion |
|---|---|---|---|---|---|---|
| | | | Left hand | Eyes | Right hand | |
| 1 | Pick up bolt | Reach for bolt. | ◡ | ⊖ ⊙→ | ⌴ | Stand by. |
| 2 | | Grasp bolt. | ∩ | | ⌴ | Stand by. |
| 3 | | Change position of bolt while carrying it to central assembly site. | ◡ + 9 | | ⌴ | Stand by. |
| 4 | Pick up nut | Hold bolt. | ⌂ | ⊖ ⊙→ | ◡ | Reach for nut. |
| 5 | | Hold bolt. | ⌂ | | ∩ | Grasp nut. |
| 6 | | Hold bolt. | ⌂ | | ◡ + 9 | Orient nut hole toward bolt while carrying nut toward bolt in left hand. |
| 7 | Assemble nut and bolt | Assemble nut and bolt. | # | | # | Assemble nut and bolt. |

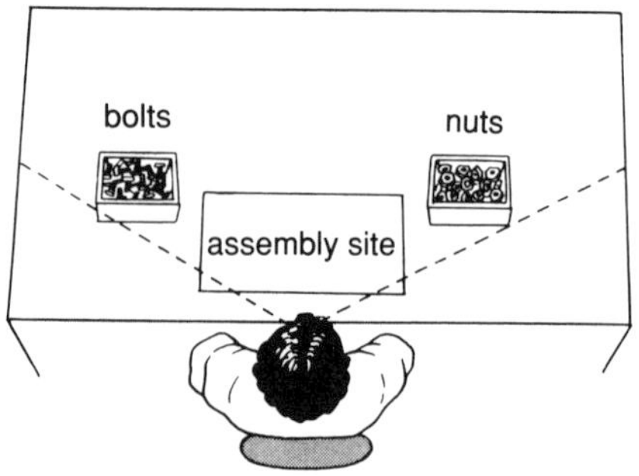


**Figure 5-5. Operation Layout (After Improvement)**

**Table 5-8. Therblig Analysis Chart (Conditions After Improvement)**

| No. | Work element | Left hand motion | Therblig | | | Right hand motion |
|---|---|---|---|---|---|---|
| | | | Left hand | Eyes | Right hand | |
| 1 | Pick up nut and bolt | Reach for bolt. | ⌣ | ◯ ◯→ | ⌣ | Reach for nut. |
| 2 | | Grasp bolt. | ∩ | | ∩ | Grasp nut. |
| 3 | | Change position of bolt while carrying it to central assembly site. | ᴗ + ᴐ | | ᴗ + ᴐ | Orient nut hole toward bolt while carrying nut toward bolt in left hand. |
| 4 | Assemble nut and bolt | Assemble nut and bolt. | ♯ | | ♯ | Assemble nut and bolt. |

*Checkpoint 3: Does the operation keep required body movements to a minimum?* Not only should all materials, parts, and tools be within the operator's field of vision, they should also be within easy reach.

In any kind of job that requires the worker to use his or her hands and arms, there is a range of easy reach in which the work can be done easily. Beyond that is a range of difficult reach that makes the job more tiring and difficult. In work study, the range of easy reach is called the "normal working area" or the "standard working area." The "maximum working area" is a range outside the normal working area that does not require moving the torso; nevertheless, it is more difficult to work in this outer area.

*Normal working area (standard working area).* For jobs that involve working on a flat surface (such as a table), the standard working area is the range of movement in which the worker can move without difficulty.

For the right hand, the normal working area is the arc made by the fingers when moving the right hand across the table. Specifically, this means moving the right arm while keeping the right elbow at the side (see Figure 5-6). The normal working area for the left hand is defined in the same way.

Often, the two arcs that define the two hands' normal working areas intersect at some point. This point determines the best site for two-handed work. Generally, the normal working area arc has a radius of about 15 inches from the worker's torso, varying somewhat with body size.

*Maximum working area.* In contrast to the normal working area, in which the worker can keep his or her elbows down, the maximum working area is defined as the arc made when the worker fully extends his or her reach, sweeping the hands across the table (see Figure 5-7). Generally, this arc has a radius of about 25 inches from the worker's torso, also varying with body size.

The intersection of the two normal working area arcs is a point where the worker can do two-handed work without too much trouble. Any motion beyond this point requires the worker to lean forward, which causes fatigue. Accordingly, you can minimize fatigue and make work more enjoyable by designing the work layout so that all objects (parts, tools, and so on) are kept within the normal working area and all two-handed work is done at or near the intersection point of that area.

One of the most important things to check when doing a therblig analysis is the common work element called *pick up object*, specifically, the sequence of motions that make up that element (reach, grasp, and transport loaded). Keep your analysis as quantitative as possible by applying the 15-inches-from-torso guideline to gauge whether this work element presents a problem. If the work element cannot be kept within this 15-inch area, it should definitely stay within the 25-inch (maximum working area) range. Figures 5-8 and 5-9 show before and after layout diagrams of an operation improvement that was made with this principle in mind.

**Figure 5-6.  Standard Working Area**

**Figure 5-7.  Maximum Working Area**

In Figure 5-8, the parts boxes are placed far out of reach. Such a layout requires the worker to lean forward for every "pick up object" work element, wasting both time and effort. By contrast, the improved layout in Figure 5-9 has both boxes arranged closer in and opening diagonally toward the worker. As explained earlier, the boxes should be within the field of vision, since this enables the worker to move the arms simultaneously and symmetrically to pick up a part from each box without difficulty.

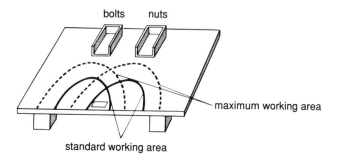

Figure 5-8. **Parts Box Layout (Before Improvement)**

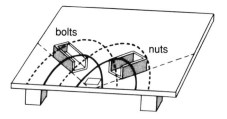

Figure 5-9. **Parts Box Layout (After Improvement)**

*Checkpoint 4: Are holding motions kept to a minimum?* If you find any hold motions in the work, start thinking of ways to eliminate them, such as by using some kind of tool or jig to do the holding instead. Also check to see whether the feet are being put to good use.

Checkpoint 1 showed how the nut-and-bolt assembly operation could be improved by making two-handed simultaneous movements that eliminate the need for one-handed holding. Developing such two-handed work is indeed the best way to eliminate holding, but when that is not possible, you should look to jigs, tools, or other devices to replace holding motions. The rule of thumb is that the hands should be used only for type 1 motions that contribute to productivity.

For an example of how a jig can be used to do the holding, see Figure 5-10, which shows the current conditions for the task of trimming bundled asparagus stalks. Table 5-9 shows the corresponding therblig analysis chart and Table 5-10 the data chart.

**Table 5-9. Therblig Analysis of Asparagus Cutting Operation (Before Improvement)**

| No. | Work element | Left hand motion | Therblig Left hand | Eyes | Therblig Right hand | Right hand motion |
|---|---|---|---|---|---|---|
| 1 | Prepare asparagus | Reach for bundle of asparagus. | ⌣ (reach) | | ⌣ (reach) | Reach for bundle of asparagus. |
| 2 | | Grasp asparagus. | ∩ (grasp) | | ∩ (grasp) | Grasp asparagus. |
| 3 | | Carry asparagus to cutting site. | ⌣ (transport loaded) | | ⌣ (transport loaded) | Carry asparagus to cutting site. |
| 4 | | Hold asparagus. | ⌂ (hold) | | ⌒ (release) | Let go of asparagus. |
| 5 | Cut end off of asparagus stalks | " | ⌂ (hold) | | ⌣ (reach) | Reach for knife. |
| 6 | | " | ⌂ (hold) | | ∩ (grasp) | Grasp knife. |
| 7 | | " | ⌂ (hold) | | ⌣ (transport loaded) | Carry knife toward bundle of asparagus. |
| 8 | | " | ⌂ (hold) | | U (use) | Cut end off of bundled asparagus stalks. |
| 9 | | " | ⌂ (hold) | | ⌣ (transport loaded) | Carry knife back to original place. |
| 10 | | " | ⌂ (hold) | | ⌒ (release) | Let go of knife. |
| 11 | Put away asparagus | " | ⌂ (hold) | | ⌣ (reach) | Reach for cut asparagus bundle. |
| 12 | | " | ⌂ (hold) | | ∩ (grasp) | Grasp bundle. |
| 13 | | Carry cut bundle to box. | ⌣ + 9 (transport loaded + position) | | ⌣ + 9 (transport loaded + position) | Carry cut bundle to box. |
| 14 | | Let go of cut bundle. | ⌒ (release) | | ⌒ (release) | Let go of cut bundle. |

**Figure 5-10. Asparagus Cutting Operation (Before Improvement)**

**Table 5-10. Summary Data Table (Before Improvement)**

|  | Therblig | Left Hand | Right Hand |
|---|---|---|---|
| Type 1 | ⌣ | 1 | 3 |
|  | ⌒ | 1 | 3 |
|  | ᴗ/ | 2 | 4 |
|  | 9 | 1 | 1 |
|  | U | — | 1 |
|  | ⌒\ | 1 | 3 |
|  | Subtotal | 6 | 15 |
| Type 3 | ⌓ | 9 | — |
| Total | | 15 | 15 |

This analysis makes it obvious that the worker's left hand performs far too many nonproductive holding motions. This led the improvement team to develop a new equipment design that made the worker's hand motions more productive. Specifically, the "cut the ends off of asparagus stalks" work element was taken over by the worker's feet, working a pedal to guide an electric saw (Figure 5-11). The only hand motions remaining were the work element "prepare asparagus." The work element "putting away the asparagus" was also simplified by a gravity-flow device that allowed the cut asparagus bundles to slide into the storage boxes automatically. Table 5-11 shows the therblig analysis chart for this improvement and Table 5-12, the summary data table.

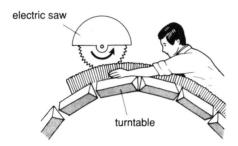

**Figure 5-11. Asparagus Cutting Operation (After Improvement)**

**Table 5-11. Therblig Analysis Chart of Asparagus Cutting Operation (After Improvement)**

| No. | Work element | Left hand motion | Therblig | | | Right hand motion |
|-----|-------------|------------------|----------|-----|------------|-------------------|
| | | | Left hand | Eyes | Right hand | |
| 1 | Prepare asparagus | Reach for bundle of asparagus. | ⌣ | | ⌣ | Reach for bundle of asparagus. |
| 2 | | Grasp asparagus. | ∩ | | ∩ | Grasp asparagus. |
| 3 | | Carry asparagus to turntable. | ⌣ | | ⌣ | Carry asparagus to turntable. |
| 4 | | Set asparagus on turntable and push toward saw blade. | ⌣ | | ⌣ | Set asparagus on turntable and push toward saw blade. (Use foot pedal to activate and stop rotary saw.) |

**Table 5-12. Summary Data Table (After Improvement)**

|  | Therblig | Left Hand | Right Hand |
|---|---|---|---|
| Type 1 | ⌣ | 1 | 1 |
|  | ⌢ | 1 | 1 |
|  | ⌣ | 2 | 2 |
| Total |  | 4 | 4 |

In just one work cycle, this improvement reduced the number of hand motions from 15 to just 4. Imagine what a difference this makes as the work cycles add up throughout the day.

*Checkpoint 5: Are the parts or materials to be processed or assembled kept where they are easy to pick up?* Keeping parts in poorly organized or hard-to-reach boxes or bins slows down the "reach for part" motion and should therefore be eliminated. That is why many factories and assembly plants use hopper bins that allow parts to fall naturally within each worker's reach.

Figure 5-12 shows a bolt box that is within easy reach, yet the worker must reach over the front of the box each time to select a bolt. Likewise, the worker must also move the hand back over the front of the box when transporting the selected bolt back to the assembly site. Table 5-13 shows the therblig analysis chart for this example.

When making a therblig analysis of this operation, it is difficult to capture such a detailed motion using only the corresponding therbligs. The "Comments" column in the expanded form of the therblig chart provides a space for you to describe and diagram the motion, as shown in Table 5-14.

This series of motions would go more smoothly if the reach-in parts box was replaced with a container that allowed the bolts to naturally drop within easier reach of the worker.

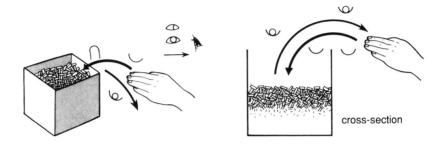

cross-section

**Figure 5-12. Picking Bolt from Parts Box**

**Table 5-13. Therblig Analysis Chart**

| No. | Left hand motion | Therblig | | | Right hand motion |
| | | Left hand | Eyes | Right hand | |
|---|---|---|---|---|---|
| 1 | Reach for bolt. | ⏑ | ◯ ◯→ | | |
| 2 | Grasp bolt. | ⋂ | | | |
| 3 | Carry bolt. | ⏑ | | | |

A study by Ralph M. Barnes examined parts bins for picking up screws or nuts from various types of bins.* Figure 5-13 depicts the three types of containers studied, (1) a gravity-feed hopper, (2) the old-style rectangular bin, and (3) a hopper with a raised tray. Timing tests showed that the hopper with the tray allowed the shortest operation time, followed by the first hopper (10 to 19 percent longer), and finally the rectangular bin (13 to 28 percent longer).

---

* *Motion and Time Study: Design and Measurement of Work*, 7th ed. (New York: John Wiley & Sons, 1980), p. 209.

**Table 5-14. Therblig Analysis Chart with Work Elements and Comments**

| No. | Work element | Left hand motion | Therblig Left hand | Therblig Eyes | Therblig Right hand | Right hand motion | Comments |
|-----|--------------|------------------|--------------------|---------------|---------------------|-------------------|----------|
| 1 | Pick up bolt | Reach for bolt. | ⌣ | 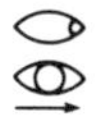 ◯ ◑→ | | | Regarding the left hand's "pick up bolt" operation:<br>• "Reach" motion is divided into two parts. |
| 2 | | Grasp bolt. | ∩ | | | | 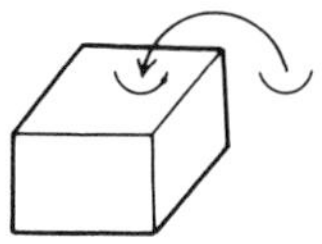 |
| 3 | | Carry bolt. | ⌣ | | | | • "Carry" motion is also divided into two parts. |

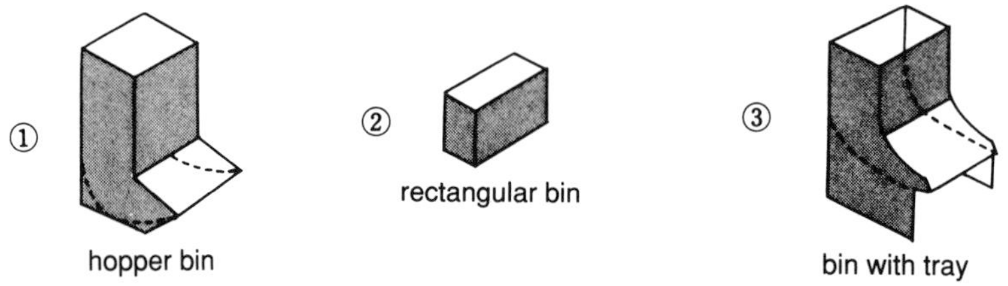

① hopper bin

② rectangular bin

③ bin with tray

Adapted from Ralph M. Barnes, *Motion and Time Study*, 7th ed. (New York: John Wiley & Sons, 1980), p. 209. Used by permission.

**Figure 5-13. Three Types of Containers**

What made the bin with the tray the quickest to use was the "knuckle space" it provided at the bottom, which made picking up parts easier. Since the parts fall naturally into the tray, the hopper is easily restocked from the top. Overall, this method eliminated the hand motions of reaching over the front of the box (i.e., the two-part reach and convey motions described in Table 5-14), which led to a much shorter operation time.

*Checkpoint 6: Are objects positioned so that they can be used as soon as they are grasped?* The idea here is to eliminate the position motion. Even though this is a type 1 motion, it is better to do without it if possible.

Consider the motions involved in writing something with a ballpoint pen. Usually, the writer keeps the pen on the desk, and the sequence of motions involved in using it are

- reach for pen
- grasp pen
- carry pen while changing its position
- use pen to write
- when finished with writing, carry pen back to original place while changing its position
- let go of pen

Table 5-15 shows a therblig analysis chart of these and other motions involved in this operation.

**Table 5-15. Therblig Analysis Chart: Using Ball-point Pen that Rests on Desktop**

| Left hand motion | Therblig | | | Right hand motion |
|---|---|---|---|---|
| | Left hand | Eyes | Right hand | |
| Reach for paper. | ⌣ | | ⌣ | Reach for ball-point pen. |
| Grasp paper. | ∩ | | ∩ | Grasp pen. |
| Hold paper. | ⌂ | | ⌒ +ᴗ | Carry pen while changing its position. |
| Hold paper. | ⌂ | | ∪ | Write words. |
| Hold paper. | ⌂ | | ⌒ +ᴗ | Carry pen back to original place while changing its position. |
| Let go of paper. | ⌒ | | ⌒ | Let go of pen (leave on desk). |

How would this series of motions change if you kept the pen in an upright pen holder instead of leaving it lying sideways on the desk? Usually, when you slide a pen out of an upright holder, you are already holding it in the position you need for writing. Accordingly, you can eliminate the position motion. When you think about it, this is one reason why upright pen holders were invented — to save people the trouble of having to position their pens for writing. Table 5-16 shows a therblig analysis chart of improved pen use with a pen holder.

**Table 5-16. Therblig Analysis Chart: Using Ball-point Pen that Rests in an Upright Pen Holder**

| Left hand motion | Therblig | | | Right hand motion |
| --- | --- | --- | --- | --- |
| | Left hand | Eyes | Right hand | |
| | | | ⌣ | Reach for ball-point pen. |
| | | | ∩ | Grasp pen. |
| | | | ⌣ | Carry pen to paper. |
| (Same as left hand motions in Table 5-15) | | | U | Write words. |
| | | | ⌣ | Carry pen back to upright pen holder. |
| | | | ⌒ | Insert pen into upright pen holder. |

This improvement saves the writer the little bit of time it takes to position the pen as he or she carries it to the paper. In therblig analysis, the use of the upright pen holder is significant also in that it eliminates the need to set up (pre-position) the pen for the next use. By eliminating the need for the pre-position motion, you have also eliminated the position motion. Thus, the introduction of a device that keeps a tool in an easier-to-use position has eliminated two motions and has thereby saved some operation time.

Consider one more example, this time involving the use of a screwdriver. As Figure 5-14 shows, the use of a device that requires the least amount of tool manipulation by keeping the tool in a ready-to-use position resulted in an impressive reduction in tool use operation time.

*Checkpoint 7: Does the operation include any unnecessary transport of assembled or processed items?* When an operation involves frequent handling of finished products (i.e., when such handling takes a lot of time), look for ways to eliminate the transport motions, such as by using chutes or other "drop delivery" devices.

By introducing a drop delivery method that allows finished (assembled or processed) products to be carried by their own weight down a ramp or chute to the product box, you can eliminate the convey product to box motion.

Another example involves burring a hole in the end of a small angle plate. Figure 5-15 shows a diagram of the operation.*

The drill is operated through the use of a foot pedal, which makes good use of the feet, a consideration noted in checkpoint 4. The angle plate to be burred is held almost exactly in the middle of the fixture and must be hand-held during the burring. The foot-operated drill can go down only to the point just beyond the angle plate, so that it never comes in contact with the work table surface below the fixture.

After the burring is finished, the operator returns the foot pedal to its original position, which raises the drill. Next, the operator releases the angle plate, whereupon it drops into the

---

* Ibid., pp. 210-11.

| | ① | ② | ③ |
|---|---|---|---|
| Grasp screwdriver, carry to screw and connect tip with screw head, turn screw, and return screwdriver to original place. |  | 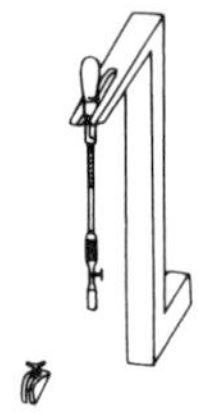 |  |
| | Lying on table | Held in stand | Hung from stand |
| Time (min.) | 0.0610 | 0.0511 | 0.0417 |
| Comparison (method 3 = 100%) | 146 | 123 | 100 |
| Therbligs | ⌣ Reach<br>∩ Grasp<br>ə+ᴗ Position while conveying<br>∪ Use<br>ᴗ+ə Position while conveying<br>⌒ Release | ⌣ Reach<br>∩ Grasp<br>ᴗ Convey<br>∪ Use<br>ᴗ Convey<br>⌒ Release | ⌣ Reach<br>∩ Grasp<br>ᴗ Convey<br>∪ Use<br>⌒ Release |
| Characteristics | Screwdriver must be positioned before and after each use. | Screwdriver must be set back into stand after each use. | Screwdriver can be simply released after each use. |

**Figure 5-14. Comparison of Screw Turning Operations Using Different Screwdriver Positions**

disposal chute via one of the holes on either side of the fixture. The burred angle plate then slides into the product box. Table 5-17 shows a therblig analysis chart of this operation.

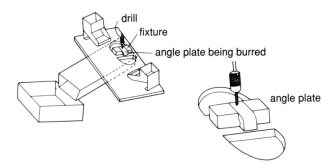

Adapted from Ralph M. Barnes, *Motion and Time Study*, 7th ed. (New York: John Wiley & Sons, 1980), p. 210.  Used by permission.

**Figure 5-15.  Angle Plate Burring Operation**

**Table 5-17.  Therblig Analysis of Burring Operation**

| Right hand motion | Therblig |
|---|---|
| Reach for angle plate in materials box at right. | ⌣ |
| Grasp angle plate in materials box at right. | ∩ |
| Carry angle plate while positioning it for fixture. | ᴜ + 9 |
| Set angle plate into fixture. | 9 |
| Hold angle plate while foot-operated drill operates. | ⌂ |
| Convey burred angle plate to product box. | ᴜ    → Use of disposal chute eliminates this motion |
| Let go of angle plate. | ⌒ |

This example underscores the importance of not being complacent about a motion simply because it belongs in type 1. Look into the content and see if anything can be eliminated. In the final analysis, the only type 1 motion that is absolutely necessary is the use (process) motion; you should look critically at all other motions as candidates for elimination. This is a good place to remind yourself of the most basic improvement-making principle, which is to look at something and ask, Why is this being done this way?

*Checkpoint 8: Do the work processes that make up the operation flow smoothly, with an easy rhythm?* Another way of putting this would be to ask whether materials and tools are laid out so that their transport is minimal (this checkpoint is thus related to checkpoint 6).

To answer this question, you must find out just what the operation's rhythm is. It may be helpful to think in terms of musical rhythms, the most familiar of which are the four-beat, three-beat, and two-beat rhythms. The four-beat rhythm is the most familiar of all, as it is used in many types of music. After that comes the three-beat rhythm, which many people identify as the waltz rhythm. Likewise, the two-beat rhythm is associated with the lively sound of the tango.

You might ask yourself what a song would sound like if it kept randomly switching among four-beat, three-beat, and two-beat rhythms. It would certainly not be very easy to listen to. The same is true of workplace operations. People can work much more pleasantly, efficiently, and with less fatigue when their manufacturing work has a smooth rhythm and is not interrupted by having to make unnecessary decisions or "change gears" psychologically.

If the materials, tools, and other items that are used in assembly or processing work are laid out well and in accordance with the work sequence, the work can be done in a smooth rhythm. If the rhythm changes from "four-beat" to "three-beat" or "two-beat" in the middle of the work sequence, workers can get confused and must stop to think about what they are doing.

Consider two motions from therblig analysis. Suppose that the worker must reach for an object that is either kept in a messy pile of assorted objects or has been moved from where it is supposed to be. This activity requires the worker to not only reach but also select, which involves some thought and can take up a lot of time.

Now consider the position motion, by which the worker sets an object in a position that paves the way for the next step in the work sequence. This motion almost always requires some mental work and planning, but the time it takes can still be shortened, as shown in the example of the upright pen holder.

As mentioned earlier, laying out the materials and tools according to the order of their use helps create a smooth work rhythm. You also need to recognize, however, that different people have different work rhythms because of their unique ways of reaching for things or grasping things.

For example, about 90 percent of the pitchers in professional baseball use the same "standard" pitching form, but the remainder have their own "irregular" ways of pitching the ball. Such variation in form is even wider among professional golfers when it comes to their swing. Just as each pitcher stands a little differently for the pitch and each golfer sets up his or her swing a little differently, so should each worker be allowed to slightly alter the positions of materials and tools to suit his or her own individual work style and rhythm.

***Checkpoint 9: Even when only one hand is used, can smooth, continuous, curved motions be used instead of straight motions that have sharp changes in direction?*** When inspecting work operations, be sure to look out for zigzag motions or motions that require sudden reversals or other sharp changes in direction.

Going back to the letter-writing example, studies have shown that a person who is writing continuously spends from 75 to 85 percent of the time actually putting ink on paper; the other 15 to 25 percent is used in moving the raised pen to start a new letter or word. The writing time is much longer when the writer writes in block print (which requires a lot of raised pen motions and sudden changes of direction) than when he or she writes in cursive (which requires much fewer raised pen motions and sudden changes of direction).

Look at an example of work rhythm improvement in a paper-folding operation (see Figure 5-16).*

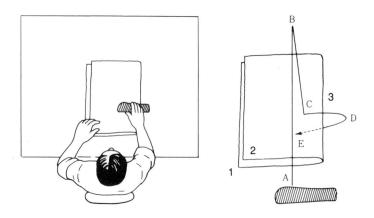

Adapted from Ralph M. Barnes, *Motion and Time Study*, 7th ed. (New York: John Wiley & Sons, 1980), p. 192. Used by permission.

**Figure 5-16. Paper Folding Operation (Before Improvement)**

The worker first picks up the right bottom edge of the paper and carries it over to meet the left bottom edge (point 1 in the figure). Next, he picks up the creasing bone and carries it to the middle of the fold (point 2 in the figure). He then presses on the bone and slides it toward the top of the folded paper (point B). At point B, he abruptly changes direction and slides

* Ibid., pp. 191-93.

the bone to point A. Next, he slides the bone back up to point B, then reverses direction and goes to point C, where he slides it sideways to point D and then back sideways the other way toward point E. Finally, he lifts the bone off the paper and the paper-folding operation is finished. Table 5-18 shows a therblig analysis chart for this operation, beginning from when the paper is aligned at point 1.

The folding operation was improved by changing the type of movement used for the creasing steps. The operation is the same as far as bringing the right edge (point 2) over to the left edge (point 1). Instead of the sharp, jerky motions for pressing the creasing bone, the improved operation uses one continuous curved motion from point X to points Y and Z, as shown in Figure 5-17. Table 5-18 shows a therblig analysis of the improved paper folding.

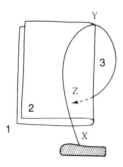

Adapted from Ralph M. Barnes, *Motion and Time Study*, 7th ed. (New York: John Wiley & Sons, 1980), p. 192. Used by permission.

**Figure 5-17. Paper Folding Operation (After Improvement)**

As Table 5-19 shows, the improved movement has greatly reduced the number of motions needed to crease the paper. In fact, the improved operation uses about 50 percent fewer creasing motions than the earlier method.

**Table 5-18. Therblig Analysis of Paper Folding Operation (Before Improvement)**

| Left hand motion | Therblig Left hand | Eyes | Therblig Right hand | Right hand motion |
|---|---|---|---|---|
| Reach for left edge (point 1). | ∪ | | ∪ | Reach for right edge (point 2). |
| Grasp (hold) left edge (point 2). | ∩ | | ∩ | Grasp right edge (point 2). |
| Hold paper at left edge (point 1). | ⌂ | | ∿ | Carry right edge (point 2) to left edge (point 1). |
| Hold paper at left edge (point 1). | ⌂ | | 9 | Match right edge (point 2) with left edge (point 1). |
| Release hand from left edge (point 1). | ↶ | | ⌂ | Hold (keep) right edge (point 2) matched with left edge (point 1). |
| Reach for right edge (point 2) on left edge (point 1). | ∪ | | ⌂ | Hold (keep) right edge (point 2) matched with left edge (point 1). |
| Grasp | ∩ | | ↶ | Release hand. |
| Hold | ⌂ | | ∪ | Reach for creasing bone. |
| " | ⌂ | | ∩ | Grasp bone. |
| " | ⌂ | | ∿ | Carry bone to point 3. |
| " | ⌂ | | ∿ | Carry (press) bone to point B. |
| " | ⌂ | | ∿ | Carry (press) bone to point A. |
| " | ⌂ | | ∿ | Carry (press) bone to point B. |
| " | ⌂ | | ∿ | Carry (press) bone to point C. |
| " | ⌂ | | ∿ | Carry (press) bone to point D. |
| " | ⌂ | | ∿ | Carry (press) bone to point E. |
| " | ⌂ | | ∿ | Let go of paper. |

### Table 5-19.  Therblig Analysis of Paper Folding Operation
### (After Improvement)

| Left hand motion | Therblig | | | Right hand motion |
|---|---|---|---|---|
| | **Left hand** | **Eyes** | **Right hand** | |
| Reach for left edge (point 1). | ∪ | | ∪ | Reach for right edge (point 2). |
| Grasp (hold) left edge (point 2). | ∩ | | ∩ | Grasp right edge (point 2). |
| Hold paper at left edge (point 1). | ⌂ | | ∾ | Carry right edge (point 2) to left edge (point 1). |
| Hold paper at left edge (point 1). | ⌂ | | 9 | Match right edge (point 2) with left edge (point 1). |
| Release hand from left edge (point 1). | ⌒ | | ⌂ | Hold (keep) right edge (point 2) matched with left edge (point 1). |
| Reach for right edge (point 2) on left edge (point 1). | ∪ | | ⌂ | " |
| Grasp | ∩ | | ⌒ | Release hand. |
| Hold | ⌂ | | ∪ | Reach for creasing bone. |
| " | ⌂ | | ∩ | Grasp bone. |
| " | ⌂ | | ∾ | Carry bone to point X. |
| " | ⌂ | | ∾ | Carry (press) bone from point X to points X and Z. |
| " | ⌂ | | ∾ | Let go of paper. |

*Checkpoint 10: Does the workplace lighting put a strain on the eyes or the work operations?* When the eyes get tired, a worker's efficiency drops and the whole body becomes fatigued. Quite often, tired eyes are due to poor lighting conditions. If the bins from which the worker must select parts or

materials are not well lit, the worker must spend more time and effort when performing the search, find, and select motions. Likewise, if the assembly site is poorly lit, the assemble and/or use motions become more tiring and time-consuming.

However, it is also possible to light up the workplace too brightly. Very brightly lit workplaces produce glare that strains the eyes, as do computer CRT displays, especially when there is glare on the CRT screen. Answering the following questions will help make sure the workplace is properly lit.

1. Is there enough light to do the work in?
2. Are the colors in the workplace subdued (not too bright)?
3. Is the light coming from the proper direction (not directly in the eyes and no glare)?

*Checkpoint 11: Are the work table and chair adjusted to the proper height to make the work easiest?* Although there are no therblig symbols to indicate these conditions, they are nonetheless important conditions to check in motion study. It is surprisingly easy to overlook simple things, such as the need to design workplaces that take into consideration the size differences among workers. Ergonomics or human factors engineering is the field of engineering that deals specifically with the issue of making the workplace more conducive to efficient and nonfatiguing human labor, whether the workers are working with machines or with other people.

A common study example for ergonomics students is the layout of an airplane cockpit. Airplanes are distinguished by the fact that they are very safe when operating normally but very unsafe when abnormal conditions occur during flight. Consequently, the cockpit layout must be carefully designed to minimize pilot fatigue and to keep all important instrumentation within the pilot's field of vision.

The same principle should apply to the factory. Factories should be designed for utmost safety and efficiency. This safety/efficiency combination is always the most important thing to check when making a motion study of factory operations. When standing workers could operate just as efficiently sitting, chairs should be provided, set at the optimum height to ensure comfort and productivity. Likewise, we should be flexible enough to realize that continuous sitting can also be fatiguing and should establish a mixture of standing and sitting operations to minimize such fatigue.

## SUMMARY OF OPERATION IMPROVEMENT USING THERBLIG ANALYSIS

You have just learned how to use therbligs in a sequence for making operation improvements. To summarize the information covered in this chapter, consider again the steps for making improvements using therblig analysis, this time within the framework of the PDCA cycle.

### Occurrence or Discovery of Problem

*Step 1: Do a PQCDSM check of the factory.* Inspect the operations, collect data, and look for problems. The PQCDSM check should include the following checkpoints:

1. Productivity (P): Has the output been sufficient?
2. Quality (Q): Are there any quality problems?
3. Cost (C): Have costs risen?
4. Delivery (D): Have deliveries been late?
5. Safety (S): Are there any safety problems?
6. Morale (M): Has the workers' morale been sinking?

*Step 2: Organize the data regarding the problem points discovered at step 1.*

### Analysis of Current Conditions

*Step 3: Determine which problems need to be addressed first.*

*Step 4: Prepare to analyze current conditions.*

1. Determine which analysis method to use (for example, you may want to use the therblig analysis method if the operations involve a lot of manual work).
2. Gather the required tools and materials, such as motion study forms, and so on.
3. Fill out the top of the analysis chart (enter the factory name, operator name, date of analysis, the chart's author, layout diagram, and so on).

*Step 5: Analyze current conditions.*

1. First, do nothing but observe the operations.
2. Take memos noting the types of motion combinations performed; later on, start noting specific motions (such as "reach for XX").
   - Note: Since it is very difficult to describe the motions in an entire operation cycle at the detailed level of a therblig analysis, begin by observing the cycle several times until you can recognize the combinations (series) of motions used. Once you have described the series of motions made by one hand, describe the other hand's motion combinations with reference to how its timing meshes with the first hand's motions.
3. Once you have made memos to describe one operation cycle, fill out the analysis chart form and enter the corresponding therbligs.
4. Interview the people who know the most about the operations and gather more data.

Apply the four principles for making improvements: study the facts as they are, be objective, use quantitative measurements and evaluations, and use symbols (such as therbligs) and graphs whenever possible to clarify information.

*Step 6: Organize the analysis results and draw up a data chart to summarize your findings.*

1. Count up the motions shown in the analysis results. Get separate subtotals for each type of therblig and for the left and right hands.
2. Also get a subtotal for the motion type categories (types 1, 2, and 3).

### Locate the Main Problem

*Step 7: Study the current-condition analysis to find which problem is most important.*

1. Find out which motions are most wasteful (types 2 and 3).
2. Check for imbalance between left-hand and right-hand motions (inconsistency and/or irrationality). At this point, be sure to check the following:
   - Check the operation conditions against the Big 3 problem checklist (see Table 3-1).
   - Check the operation conditions against the 5W1H checklist (see Table 3-4) and emphasize the Why? question.
   - Do a PQCDSM check (see Table 3-3).
   - Apply the principles of motion economy (see the checkpoints described earlier in this chapter).

### Draft an Improvement Plan

*Step 8: Look carefully at the current conditions to identify motions that can be eliminated.*

1. Looking at the problems discovered via the current-condition analysis and at other suspicious motions or

operations, ask, Why must this be done this way? Try to eliminate all extraneous motions, including type 1 motions.

2. Hold a brainstorming session to come up with suggestions and ideas.

*Step 9: Once you have finished trying to eliminate motions, use the other three improvement principles to improve the remaining motions:*

1. Look for ways to simplify them.
2. Look for ways to combine operations economically.
3. Look for ways to improve things by changing the work sequence.

*Step 10: Repeat steps 8 and 9 in brainstorming sessions to come up with improvement plans. It is good to come up with several alternative plans for discussion and comparison.*

1. Improvement plans fall into three categories:
   - Plan 1: Can be implemented right away
   - Plan 2: Requires some preparation
   - Plan 3: Requires a lot of preparation
2. Create therblig analysis charts and data summary charts for before-improvement and predicted after-improvement data to compare the expected benefits of the various plans.

When drafting an improvement plan, keep in mind the fourfold purpose of making improvements: to make the operations go easier, better, less expensively, and faster. Finally, evaluate your alternative plans using:

- the 5W1H checklist (see Table 3-4)
- the improvement concerns (see therbligs and checkpoints in Table 5-20)
- the principles of motion economy

*Step 11: Select a final plan and give it a feasibility test (trial implementation).*

*Step 12: If it seems the plan will work, check with the various people who are directly affected by its implementation.*

*Step 13: Once all preparations are finished, implement the improvement plan.*

### Occurrence or Discovery of Problem

Improvements come in cycles; now it is time to go back to the start of this cycle and begin another round of improvement making.

## Table 5-20.  Therblig Symbols and Corresponding Checkpoints

**Type 1: Motions required for performing an operation**

| | Motion | Therblig | Checkpoints |
|---|---|---|---|
| 1 | Transport Empty | ⌣ TE | 1. Can items be arranged to minimize the distance of "transport empty" motions?<br>2. Are there any items that interfere and require a change of direction in the "transport empty" motion?<br>3. Is there a smooth path to the object? |
| 2 | Grasp | ⋂ G | 1. Is it possible to grasp more than one object at once to reduce the number of grasp motions?<br>2. Can small objects that are difficult to grasp be slid instead of carried?<br>3. Can any right-hand operations be transferred to the left hand, and can any hand operations be transferred to a foot? |
| 3 | Transport Loaded | ⌣ TL | 1. Are objects laid out so as to minimize the transportation distance?<br>2. Can a conveyor chute be used to replace hand transport?<br>3. Can a motorized conveyor be used to replace hand transport?<br>4. Can a foot-operated device be used to replace hand transport?<br>5. Is there a way to avoid subsequent motions that slow down the transport step, such as making adjustments in a carrying position?<br>6. Is transport speed slowed by an obstacle?<br>7. Are the path and/or the required body positions awkward?<br>8. Does the transport motion involve any unnecessary body motions?<br>9. Are the hands moving simultaneously and symmetrically? |
| 4 | Position | 9 P | 1. Can the need for positioning be eliminated?<br>2. Are tools and parts kept in a neat, orderly arrangement?<br>3. Are there items that should be lined up neatly but are not?<br>4. Can a hopper bin or chute be used to eliminate positioning? |

**Type 1:  Motions required for performing an operation (cont.)**

| | Motion | Therblig | Checkpoints |
|---|---|---|---|
| 5 | Assemble | ⧻ <br> A | 1. Can a stopper or guide mechanism be used to facilitate assembly? <br> 2. Is there a way to assemble more than one product at a time? |
| 6 | Disassemble | ⧻ <br> DA | 1. Can a jig, fixture, or automated mechanism be used to facilitate or eliminate manual disassembly? <br> 2. Can several items be taken apart at the same time? <br> 3. Can a tool be used to facilitate disassembly? |
| 7 | Use | ∪ <br> U | 1. Is there a jig, fixture, or automated mechanism that can facilitate or eliminate the "use" motion? <br> 2. Can several items be used at the same time? <br> 3. Can an easier-to-use tool be used instead? <br> 4. Is there a way to automatically dispose of cut debris during cutting? <br> 5. Can mechanized devices be used to save labor? |
| 8 | Release | ⌒ <br> RL | 1. Is there a device that can get the release object to the right place without the operator's specific attention? <br> 2. Can a drop delivery device be used to catch released items? <br> 3. Can the item be released while being carried (i.e., during a transport motion)? <br> 4. Can a mechanism or pressurized system be used to mechanically release the item? |
| 9 | Inspect | ◊ <br> I | 1. Can the inspect motion be eliminated or at least abbreviated? <br> 2. Can several items be inspected at the same time? |

**Type 2: Motions that tend to slow down Type 1 motion**

| | Motion | Therblig | Checkpoints |
|---|---|---|---|
| 10 | Search | Sh | 1. Are materials, parts, and tools laid out clearly so they do not need to be searched for?<br>2. Are materials, parts, and tools kept at similar distances? (The eyes get tired if they have to focus on objects at various distances.)<br>3. Are all eye movements lateral rather than vertical? |
| 11 | Find | F | 1. Are the material bins, parts, and tools arranged by shape and color in a way that makes them easy to find? |
| 12 | Select | St | 1. Are parts, materials, and tools laid out separately, or are they mixed in together?<br>2. Can items be laid out in a way that eliminates the need for the search-find-select sequence? |
| 13 | Plan | Pn | 1. Can planning tasks be made more concrete (i.e., less thought required)? |
| 14 | Pre-position | PP | 1. Can a stopper or guide mechanism be used to eliminate the need for pre-positioning?<br>2. Can tools be hung from fixtures for automatic pre-positioning?<br>3. Can tools be arranged or modified to make them easier to pick up? |

**Type 3: Motions that do not perform an operation**

| | Motion | Therblig | Checkpoints |
|---|---|---|---|
| 15 | Hold | $\bigcap$ <br> H | 1. Is there a way to eliminate the hold motion? <br> 2. Can other things be used for holding instead of the hands (e.g., feet, vises, holders, and so on)? |
| 16 | Unavoidable delay | $\wedge$ <br> UD | 1. Can motions be combined or changed to eliminate delays? <br> 2. If the delay is due to poor management or another worker's actions, can the problem be corrected? |
| 17 | Avoidable delay | $\smile$ <br> AD | 1. Is there a way to eliminate such delays? <br> 2. Can conditions at the previous or subsequent process be improved to eliminate the delay? |
| 18 | Rest | $\stackrel{?}{\smile}$ <br> R | 1. Have rest periods been well planned? <br> 2. Can work posture be alternated (standing, sitting, etc.) to prevent fatigue? <br> 3. Is there a way to help workers recover from fatigue more quickly? |

# 6

# Motion Improvement
# Case Studies

Chapters 4 and 5 focused on the motion study method known as therblig analysis. This chapter presents two case studies that show how this method can be used in making effective improvements (see outline in Table 6-1). These interesting examples were presented during the JUSE basic course on industrial engineering for factory managers.

These case studies are presented to help you understand the key aspects of making improvements; the details of the specific situations are relatively unimportant. Specifically, the two case studies demonstrate the importance of the following three axioms of motion study:

1. Carefully and objectively observe the current conditions.
2. Dig deep to discover the true problem points.
3. Put the principles of improvement making and motion economy to effective use.

**Table 6-1. Outline of Motion Study Case Studies**

| Improvement theme | Company/ person's name | Main method used | Summary |
|---|---|---|---|
| 1. Improvement of glass assembly process | Ricoh Watch Co., Ltd./ Toshio Asai | Motion study (therblig analysis) | They made a therblig analysis of the glass assembly process on the water meter assembly line and fully applied the principles of motion economy to do the following:<br>• Established two-handed (simultaneous) motions<br>• Developed holding devices to aid assembly<br>• Improved the layout of parts bins |
| 2. Improvement of steel cord welding machine operations for steel radial tires | Bridgestone Becalt Steel Cord Co., Ltd./ Sadakatsu Tezuka | Four principles (especially "combination") of improvements using motion study (therblig analysis) | They did a therblig analysis of the operations involved in this process, which consisted mainly of the following post-welding operations:<br>• hammering<br>• width inspection<br>• bending inspection<br>• strength test<br>• curing test<br><br>Applying the four principles of improvement-making, they combined processes and automated to improve manual processes. |

## CASE STUDY 1: IMPROVEMENT OF A GLASS ASSEMBLY PROCESS

Toshio Asai works in the gauge operations division at Ricoh Watch Company, which produces water meters, gas meters, and copy machines. His current duties include supervising assembly operations in department 1 on the water meter production line.

Figure 6-1 illustrates the parts used in the water meter assembly process. These parts include a bottom casing, into which an inner pipe, display mechanism, magnet assembly, and glass assembly are inserted. Finally, a top casing is screwed onto the inserted parts to complete the meter assembly process. Table 6-2 shows a process analysis chart of this water meter production process.

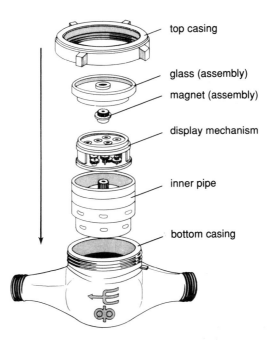

**Figure 6-1. Water Meter Assembly**

Department 1 has three sections: the machining section, where the bottom casing is machined; the assembly section, where the water meter is assembled; and the inspection section, where the assembled meter is performance-tested. Asai is the immediate supervisor for the assembly section.

**Table 6-2. Process Chart of Water Meter Production (Outline)**

| Flow chart | | | Process name |
|---|---|---|---|
| Raw materials process | Setup process | Main process | |
| | | | Machining of bottom casing |
| | | | Insert inner pipe |
| | | | Insert display mechanism |
| | | | Insert magnet assembly |
| | | | Insert glass assembly |
| | | | Fasten top casing |
| | | | Performance inspection |

**Table 6-3. Organization of PQCDSM Data**

| | Checkpoint | Yes/No | Description |
|---|---|---|---|
| P (Productivity) | Are there any problems in output volume? | Yes | A lot of the work is being done with one hand idle. Maybe a more efficient two-handed method can be devised. |
| Q (Quality) ⋮ | Are there any quality problems? ⋮ | No ⋮ | No quality problems ⋮ |

The most time-consuming part of the assembly operation is assembling the display mechanism. Asai and the other assembly workers thought that there must be a more efficient way to assemble it. After studying the problem for a while, they realized that improving the display mechanism would probably be a very complicated matter. Therefore, they decided to start their improvement efforts with a simpler target, the glass assembly process.

## Discovering the Problem

### Step 1: Study of Daily Operations and Identification of Items in Need of Improvement

The group conducted a PQCDSM check for the glass assembly process and came up with the following detailed description of that process:

1. *Glass holder pipe preparation.* On the work table, line up a row of the holder pipes that will fit into the center holes of the glass plates.
2. *Insert "A" washers.* Insert one of the bottom ("A") washers onto each of the holder pipes.
3. *Insert glass plates.* Insert a glass plate onto each of the holder pipes.
4. *Insert "B" washers.* Insert the top ("B") washers for the nut that will fasten down the glass plate.
5. *Line up nuts.* Set a nut on top of each glass holder pipe.
6. *Fasten nuts.* Turn the nuts onto the holder pipe screw threads to fasten down the glass plate.
7. *Put away products.* Stack the finished glass assemblies into two stacks of four.

### Step 2: Collection of Data Obtained from PQCDSM Check and Arrangement of Data in a Table (see Table 6-3)

## Analyzing Current Conditions

### Step 3: Selection of Problem for Improvement

As mentioned above, the workers suspected that the main improvement need concerned the display mechanism assembly process, but since that is such a complicated process, they decided to first analyze and improve the glass assembly process.

### Step 4: Preparation for Analysis of Current Conditions

The improvement team prepared to do a current-condition analysis of the glass assembly process.

1. Since this process includes a lot of manual operations, they decided to use therblig analysis for their current-condition analysis.
2. They got out a therblig analysis form and set it up for their analysis (see Table 6-4).

**Table 6-4. Therblig Analysis Form (partial)**

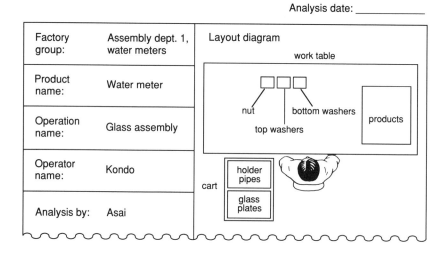

### Step 5: Analysis of Current Conditions

First, the group observed several repetitions of the glass assembly operation cycle. Gradually, they gained a better understanding of what was really going on in the operation and in what order. After they were familiar with the various detailed aspects of the operations, they started noting the general flow of the glass assembly process and drew rough illustrations of every stage up to completion. Their analysis results included the following points:

1. The assembly worker lines up eight glass holder pipes by taking four pipes out of the parts bin two times (see Figure 6-2).
2. He reaches with his left hand to pick out some "A" washers from the parts bin, then uses his right hand to lay washers onto the glass holder pipes (see Figure 6-3).

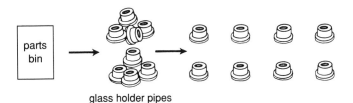

glass holder pipes

**Figure 6-2. Current-condition Analysis (1): Glass Holder Pipes**

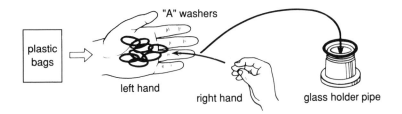

**Figure 6-3. Current-condition Analysis (2): Bottom ("A") Washers**

3. He reaches with his left hand and picks up three glass plates from the parts bin and then uses his right hand to set them onto the holder pipes. After completing the first three glass plates, he does the same for another three, then for the last two, making a total of eight glass plate/holder assemblies (see Figure 6-4).

4. He reaches with his left hand to pick out some "B" washers from the parts bin, then uses his right hand to lay washers onto the glass plates. He does this for all eight glass plate/holder assemblies (see Figure 6-5).

5. Next, he reaches with his left hand and picks out some nuts from the parts bin. He uses his right hand to place a nut on top of the holder pipe in each of the eight glass plate/holder assemblies (see Figure 6-6).

6. He tightens the nuts to fasten down each of the eight glass plate-holder assemblies (see Figure 6-7).

7. Last, he stacks the completed glass assemblies into two stacks of four (see Figure 6-8).

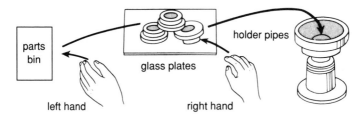

**Figure 6-4. Current-condition Analysis (3): Glass Plates**

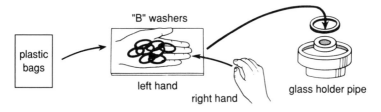

**Figure 6-5. Current-condition Analysis (4): Top ("B") Washers**

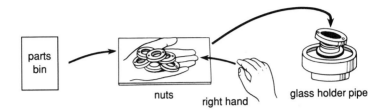

**Figure 6-6.  Current-condition Analysis (5): Nuts**

**Figure 6-7.  Current-condition Analysis (6): Tightening Nuts**

**Figure 6-8.  Current-condition Analysis (7):
Stacking Completed Assemblies**

### Step 6: Completion of the Therblig Analysis Chart

While the information is still fresh, the group filled in a therblig analysis chart using the data they had noted down and what they had seen and memorized.

After filling out the therblig analysis chart, they counted the different types of therbligs and organized them into a data chart and then drew up a Pareto chart as a graphic data summary. Table 6-5 shows their completed therblig analysis chart.

## Finding the Most Important Problems

### Step 7: Study of the Analysis Results to Determine Which Problem Is Most Important

The team performed a check based on the principles of motion economy and determined that the following problems warranted the most attention:

1. *There are too many type 2 and type 3 motions.* As the group's data chart and Pareto chart show (see Table 6-6 and Figure 6-9), there are many hold and unavoidable delay (standby) activities, both of which are type 3 motions. There are also a lot of pre-position (setup) motions, which are type 2 motions.
2. The left-hand and right-hand motions are not balanced. In other words, they are not simultaneous two-handed motions.
   - The left hand has too many hold motions. The left hand spends too much time holding things while the right hand works.
   - The right hand has too many standby motions. This means that the right hand is not used often enough.
3. As the layout diagram shows, the parts and materials bins are laid out poorly (see Table 6-4).

## Table 6-5.  Therblig Analysis Chart (Before Improvement)

| No. | Work element | Left hand motion | Therblig | | | Right hand motion | Notes |
|---|---|---|---|---|---|---|---|
| | | | Left | Eyes | Right | | |
| 1 | Set up glass holder pipes | Reach for holder pipes. | ∪ | ⊖ ⊕ | ∧ | Stand by | |
| 2 | | Grasp holder pipes. | ∩ | | ∧ | " | |
| 3 | | Carry holder pipes to work table. | ⌣ | | ∧ | " | |
| 4 | | Set down holder pipes. | ⌒ | | ∧ | " | |
| 5 | | Repeat above motions. | ∪ | ⊖ ⊕ | ∧ | " | |
| 6 | | | ∩ | | ∧ | " | |
| 7 | | | ⌣ | | ∧ | " | |
| 8 | | | ⌒ | | ∧ | " | |
| 9 | | Reach for holder pipe on work table. | ∪ | | ∪ | Same as left hand motion. | |
| 10 | | Grasp holder pipe. | ∩ | | ∩ | | |
| 11 | | Carry holder pipe. | ⌣ | | ⌣ | | |
| 12 | | Line up holder pipe. | 9 | | 9 | | |
| 13 | | Let go of holder pipe. | ⌒ | | ⌒ | | |
| 14 | | Repeat above motions. | ∪ | | ∪ | " | |
| 15 | | | ∩ | | ∩ | | |
| 16 | | | ⌣ | | ⌣ | | |
| 17 | | | 9 | | 9 | | |
| 18 | | | ⌒ | | ⌒ | | |

## Table 6-5. Therblig Analysis Chart (Before Improvement) (cont'd)

| No. | Work element | Left hand motion | Therblig Left | Therblig Eyes | Therblig Right | Right hand motion | Notes |
|---|---|---|---|---|---|---|---|
| 19 | Set up holder pipes | Repeat same motions. | ⌣ | | ⌣ | Same as left hand motions. | |
| 20 | | | ∩ | | ∩ | | |
| 21 | | | ⌣ | | ⌣ | | |
| 22 | | | 9 | | 9 | | |
| 23 | | | ⌢ | | ⌢ | | |
| 24 | | " | ⌣ | | ⌣ | " | |
| 25 | | | ∩ | | ∩ | | |
| 26 | | | ⌣ | | ⌣ | | |
| 27 | | | 9 | | 9 | | |
| 28 | | | ⌢ | | ⌢ | | |
| 29 | Insert "A" washers | Reach for the "A" washers. | ⌣ | | ⌁ | Stand by. | |
| 30 | | Grasp some "A" washers. | ∩ | | ⌁ | " | |
| 31 | | Carry "A" washers. | ⌣ | | ⌁ | " | |
| 32 | | Hold "A" washers. | ⌂ | | ⌁ | " | |
| 33 | | Hold "A" washers. | ⌂ | | ⌣ | Reach for an "A" washer in left hand. | |
| 34 | | " | ⌂ | | ∩ | Grasp an "A" washer in left hand. | |
| 35 | | " | ⌂ | | ⌣ | Carry "A" washer to holder pipe. | |
| 36 | | " | ⌂ | | 9 | Set "A" washer on holder pipe. | |
| 37 | | " | ⌂ | | ♯ | Insert "A" washer into groove in holder pipe. | |
| 38 | | " | ⌂ | | ⌢ | Let go of "A" washer. | |

## Table 6-5. Therblig Analysis Chart (Before Improvement) (cont'd)

| No. | Work element | Left hand motion | Therblig Left | Therblig Eyes | Therblig Right | Right hand motion | Notes |
|---|---|---|---|---|---|---|---|
| 39 | Insert "A" washers | Hold "A" washers in palm. | ⌂ | | ‿ | | |
| 40 | | " | ⌂ | | ∩ | Repeat above motions. | |
| 41 | | " | ⌂ | | ᴗ | | |
| 42 | | " | ⌂ | | ୨ | | |
| 43 | | " | ⌂ | | ♯ | | |
| 44 | | " | ⌂ | | ⌒ | | |
| 75 | | Hold "A" washers in palm. | ⌂ | | ‿ | Repeat above motions (until eighth washer is done). | |
| 76 | | " | ⌂ | | ∩ | | |
| 77 | | Return remaining "A" washers. | ᴗ | | ᴗ | | |
| 78 | | Let go of "A" washers. | ⌒ | | ୨ | | |
| 79 | | Stand by. | ⌁ | | ♯ | | |
| 80 | | " | ⌁ | | ⌒ | | |
| 81 | Insert glass plates | Reach for glass plates. | ‿ | ⊙ ⊙↓ | ⌁ | Stand by. | |
| 82 | | Grasp glass plates. | ∩ | | ⌁ | " | |
| 83 | | Carry glass plates. | ᴗ | | ⌁ | " | |
| 84 | | Hold glass plates. | ⌂ | | ‿ | Reach for glass plate in left hand. | |
| 85 | | " | ⌂ | | ∩ | Grasp glass plate. | |
| 86 | | " | ⌂ | | ᴗ | Carry glass plate to holder pipe. | |
| 87 | | " | ⌂ | | 8 | Check direction. | |
| 88 | | " | ⌂ | | ୨ | Align glass with holder pipe. | |
| 89 | | " | ⌂ | | ♯ | Insert glass onto holder pipe. | |
| 90 | | " | ⌂ | | ⌒ | Let go of assembly. | |

### Table 6-5. Therblig Analysis Chart (Before Improvement) (cont'd)

| No. | Work element | Left hand motion | Therblig Left | Therblig Eyes | Therblig Right | Right hand motion | Notes |
|-----|--------------|------------------|------|------|-------|-------------------|-------|
| 91 | Insert glass plates | Hold glass plates. | ⌓ | | ⌣ | Insert glass plate (second one). | |
| 92 | | " | ⌓ | | ∩ | | |
| 93 | | " | ⌓ | | ⌣ | | |
| 94 | | " | ⌓ | | 8 | | |
| 95 | | " | ⌓ | | 9 | | |
| 96 | | " | ⌓ | | # | | |
| 97 | | " | ⌓ | | ⌒ | | |
| 98 | | Hold glass plates. | ⌓ | | ⌣ | Stand by. | |
| 99 | | " | ⌓ | | ∩ | | |
| 100 | | Insert glass plate (third one). | ⌢ | | ⌣ | | |
| 101 | | " | ⌢ | | 8 | | |
| 102 | | " | ⌢ | | 9 | | |
| 103 | | " | ⌢ | | # | | |
| 104 | | " | ⌢ | | ⌒ | | |
| 105 | | Reach for glass plates. | ⌣ | ⊙ | ⌢ | Stand by. | |
| 106 | | Grasp glass plates. | ∩ | | ⌢ | " | |
| 107 | | Carry glass plates. | ⌣ | | ⌢ | " | |
| 108 | | Hold glass plates. | ⌓ | | ⌣ | Insert glass plate (fourth one). | |
| 109 | | " | ⌓ | | ∩ | | |
| 110 | | " | ⌓ | | ⌣ | | |
| 111 | | " | ⌓ | | 8 | | |
| 112 | | " | ⌓ | | 9 | | |
| 113 | | " | ⌓ | | # | | |
| 114 | | " | ⌓ | | ⌒ | | |

## Table 6-5. Therblig Analysis Chart (Before Improvement) (cont'd)

| No. | Work element | Left hand motion | Therblig Left | Therblig Eyes | Therblig Right | Right hand motion | Notes |
|---|---|---|---|---|---|---|---|
| 129 | Insert glass plates | Reach for glass plates. | ⌣ | ◯ ⬭→ | ⌒ | Stand by. | |
| 130 | | Grasp glass plates. | ∩ | | ⌒ | " | |
| 131 | | Carry glass plates. | ⌣ | | ⌒ | " | |
| 132 | | Hold glass plates. | ⌂ | | ⌣ | Insert glass plate (seventh one). | |
| 133 | | " | ⌂ | | ∩ | | |
| 134 | | " | ⌂ | | ⌣ | | |
| 135 | | " | ⌂ | | 𝟪 | | |
| 136 | | " | ⌂ | | 𝟫 | | |
| 137 | | " | ⌂ | | ♯ | | |
| 138 | | " | ⌂ | | ⌒ | | |
| 139 | | Hold glass plates. | ⌂ | | ⌣ | Insert glass plate (eighth one). | |
| 140 | | " | ⌂ | | ∩ | | |
| 141 | | Stand by. | ⌒ | | ⌣ | | |
| 142 | | " | ⌒ | | 𝟪 | | |
| 143 | | " | ⌒ | | 𝟫 | | |
| 144 | | " | ⌒ | | ♯ | | |
| 145 | | " | ⌒ | | ⌒ | | |
| 146 | Insert "B" washers | Reach for the "B" washers. | ⌣ | | ⌒ | Stand by. | |
| 147 | | Grasp some "B" washers. | ∩ | | ⌒ | " | |
| 148 | | Carry "B" washers. | ⌣ | | ⌒ | " | |
| 149 | | Hold "B" washers. | ⌂ | | ⌒ | " | |

**Table 6-5. Therblig Analysis Chart (Before Improvement) (cont'd)**

| No. | Work element | Left hand motion | Therblig Left | Therblig Eyes | Therblig Right | Right hand motion | Notes |
|---|---|---|---|---|---|---|---|
| 150 | Insert "B" washer | Hold "B" washers in palm. | ⌂ | | ◡ | Reach for a "B" washer in left hand. | |
| 151 | | " | ⌂ | | ∩ | Grasp a "B" washer in left hand. | |
| 152 | | " | ⌂ | | ◡o | Carry "B" washer to holder pipe. |  |
| 153 | | " | ⌂ | | 9 | Set "B" washer on holder pipe. | |
| 154 | | " | ⌂ | | # | Insert "B" washer into groove in holder pipe. | |
| 155 | | " | ⌂ | | ⌒o | Let go of "B" washer. | |
| 192 | | Hold "B" washers in palm. | ⌂ | | ◡ | Repeat above motions (until eighth washer is done). | |
| 193 | | " | ⌂ | | ∩ | | |
| 194 | | Return remaining "B" washers. | ◡o | | ◡o | | |
| 195 | | Let go of "B" washers. | ⌒o | | 9 | | |
| 196 | | Stand by. | ^o | | # | | |
| 197 | | " | ^o | | ⌒o | | |
| 198 | Set up nuts | Reach for some nuts. | ◡ | | ^o | Carry nuts. | |
| 199 | | Stand by. | ∩ | | ^o | " |  |
| 200 | | Grasp some nuts. | ◡o | | ^o | " | |
| 201 | | Hold nuts. | ⌂ | | ◡ | Reach for nut in left hand. | |
| 202 | | " | ⌂ | | ∩ | Grasp nut. | |
| 203 | | " | ⌂ | | ◡o | Carry nut. | |
| 204 | | " | ⌂ | | 8 | Check direction of nut. |  |
| 205 | | " | ⌂ | | 9 | Line nut up on holder pipe. | |
| 206 | | " | ⌂ | | ⌒o | Set nut down on holder pipe. | |

## Table 6-5. Therblig Analysis Chart (Before Improvement) (cont'd)

| No. | Work element | Left hand motion | Therblig Left | Therblig Eyes | Therblig Right | Right hand motion | Notes |
|---|---|---|---|---|---|---|---|
| 207 | Set up nuts | Hold nuts. | ⌓ | | ⌣ | Repeat above motions (for second nut). | |
| 208 | | " | ⌓ | | ∩ | | |
| 209 | | " | ⌓ | | ⌣ | | |
| 243 | | Hold nuts. | ⌓ | | ⌣ | Repeat above motions (up to eight nuts). | |
| 244 | | " | ⌓ | | ∩ | | |
| 245 | | Return remaining nuts. | ⌣ | | ⌣ | | |
| 246 | | Let go of nuts. | ⌒ | | 8 | | |
| 247 | | Stand by. | ⌁ | | 9 | | |
| 248 | | " | ⌁ | | ⌒ | | |
| 249 | Fasten nut | Reach for holder pipe. | ⌣ | | ⌣ | Reach for nut. | |
| 250 | | Grasp holder pipe. | ∩ | | ∩ | Grasp nut. | |
| 251 | | Hold holder pipe. | ⌓ | | ♯ | Screw on nut. | |
| 252 | | Let go of holder pipe. | ⌒ | | ⌒ | Let go of nut. | |
| 253 | | Repeat above motions (for second holder pipe). | ⌣ | | ⌣ | Repeat above motions (for second nut). | |
| 254 | | | ∩ | | ∩ | | |
| 255 | | | ⌓ | | ♯ | | |
| 256 | | | ⌒ | | ⌒ | | |
| 257 | | Repeat above motions (for third holder pipe). | ⌣ | | ⌣ | Repeat above motions (for third nut). | |
| 258 | | | ⌓ | | ♯ | | |
| 259 | | | ⌒ | | ⌒ | | |
| 260 | | | | | | | |

## Table 6-5.  Therblig Analysis Chart (Before Improvement) (cont'd)

| No. | Work element | Left hand motion | Therblig Left | Therblig Eyes | Therblig Right | Right hand motion | Notes |
|---|---|---|---|---|---|---|---|
| 281 | Stack products (glass assem- blies) | Stand by. | ⌒ | | ⌣ | Reach for four glass assemblies. | |
| 282 | | " | ⌒ | | ∩ | Grasp glass assembly. | |
| 283 | | " | ⌒ | | ⌣ | Carry glass assembly. | |
| 284 | | " | ⌒ | | ⌒ | Stack glass assembly. | |
| 285 | | " | ⌒ | | ⌣ | Repeat above motions (for second glass assembly). | |
| 286 | | " | ⌒ | | ∩ | | |
| 287 | | " | ⌒ | | ⌣ | | |
| 288 | | " | ⌒ | | ⌒ | | |
| 289 | | " | ⌒ | | ⌣ | Repeat above motions (for third glass assembly). | |
| 290 | | " | ⌒ | | ∩ | | |
| 291 | | " | ⌒ | | ⌣ | | |
| 292 | | " | ⌒ | | ⌒ | | |
| 293 | | " | ⌒ | | ⌣ | Repeat above motions (for fourth glass assembly). | |
| 294 | | " | ⌒ | | ∩ | | |
| 295 | | Reach for four more glass assemblies. | ⌣ | | ⌣ | | |
| 296 | | Grasp glass assemblies. | ∩ | | ⌒ | | |
| 297 | | Carry glass assemblies. | ⌣ | | ⌣ | Repeat above motions (for fifth glass assembly). | |
| 298 | | Hold glass assemblies. | ⌂ | | ∩ | | |
| 299 | | Repeat same motions (for sixth glass assembly). | ⌣ | | ⌣ | | |
| 300 | | | ∩ | | ⌒ | | |

**Table 6-5. Therblig Analysis Chart (Before Improvement) (cont'd)**

| No. | Work element | Left hand motion | Therblig Left | Eyes | Right | Right hand motion | Notes |
|---|---|---|---|---|---|---|---|
| 301 | Stack products (glass assemblies) | Repeat same motions (for seventh glass assembly). | ⌣⟋ |  | ⌣ | Repeat same motions (for sixth glass assembly). |  |
| 302 |  |  | ⌂ |  | ∩ |  |  |
| 303 |  |  | ⌣ |  | ⌣⟋ |  |  |
| 304 |  |  | ∩ |  | ⌢ |  |  |
| 305 |  | Repeat same motions (for eighth glass assembly). | ⌣⟋ |  | ⌣ | Repeat same motions (for seventh glass assembly). |  |
| 306 |  |  | ⌂ |  | ∩ |  |  |
| 307 |  |  | ⌣ |  | ⌣⟋ |  |  |
| 308 |  |  | ∩ |  | ⌢ |  |  |
| 309 |  |  | ⌣⟋ |  | ⌣ | Repeat same motions (for eighth glass assembly). |  |
| 310 |  |  | ⌂ |  | ∩ |  |  |
| 311 |  | Stand by. | ⌃∘ |  | ⌣⟋ |  |  |
| 312 |  | " | ⌃∘ |  | ⌢ |  |  |

**Table 6-6. Data Chart**

| Type | 1 | | | | | | | | | | 2 | | | | | | 3 | | | | | Total |
|---|---|---|---|---|---|---|---|---|---|---|---|---|---|---|---|---|---|---|---|---|---|---|---|
| Therblig | ⌣ | ∩ | ⌣⟋ | ⧢ | ⇈ | ↔ | ∪ | ⌢ | ◯ | No. | ◯ | ⊂⊃ | → | ୧ | δ | No. | ⌂ | ⌃ | ⌣⟍ | ⌐ | No. |  |
| Left hand | 24 | 24 | 18 | 4 |  |  | 18 |  |  | 88 |  |  |  |  | — | 187 | 37 |  |  | 224 | 312 |  |
| Right hand | 52 | 52 | 44 | 36 | 32 |  | 52 |  |  | 268 |  |  | 16 | 16 |  |  | 28 |  |  | 28 | 312 |  |
| Eyes |  |  |  |  |  |  |  | 5 | 5 | 5 |  | 15 |  |  |  |  |  |  |  |  | 15 |  |

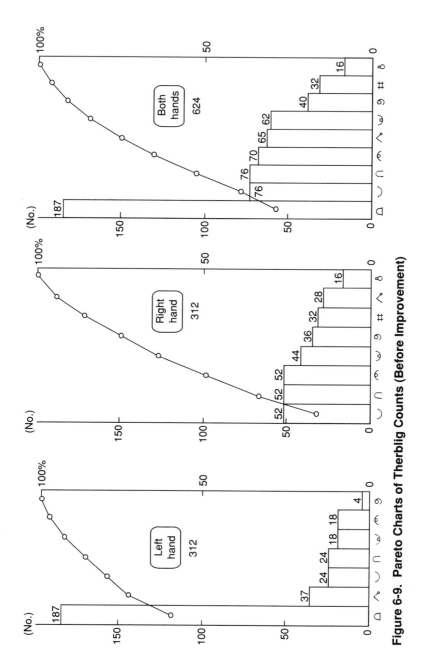

**Figure 6-9. Pareto Charts of Therblig Counts (Before Improvement)**

## Drafting Improvement Plans

### Step 8: Formulation of Improvement Plans to Eliminate Motions

### Step 9: Use of the Improvement-making Principles of Simplification, Combination, and Replacement in Devising the Improvement Plans

The group followed steps 8 and 9 and tried to come up with a good improvement plan.

### Step 10: Selection of an Improvement Plan

*Establishing simultaneous two-handed motions (checkpoint 1 in motion economy principles).* The group had found at step 7 that the operations did not use many simultaneous two-handed motions. This led them to apply two of the four principles for making improvements, namely:

- Eliminate hold motions
- Eliminate standby motions

The group looked at the operation layout again and noticed that the parts bins containing the holder pipe and the glass plates are down by the assembly worker's left hip, as shown on the left side of Figure 6-10. This position, plus the fact that they are kept in loose piles, makes picking up these parts difficult and tiring. It also requires the search-find-select series of motions. They also noticed that having all of the parts bins on one side of the assembly worker made it impossible for him to pick up the parts using both hands at once.

They improved this layout by arranging the parts boxes on both sides and at a higher position, as shown on the right side of Figure 6-10. They also arranged to have the parts neatly stacked at the previous process. As a result of this improvement, the assembly worker was able to pick up parts from both sides

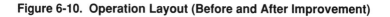

"A" washers
"B" washers
(plastic bags)
holder pipes
glass plates

Before: Set low and on one side only     After: Set higher and on both sides

**Figure 6-10.  Operation Layout (Before and After Improvement)**

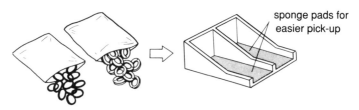

sponge pads for
easier pick-up

Before: Washers kept in plastic bags     After: Washers kept in parts bins

**Figure 6-11.  Improvement of Washer Pick-up Method**

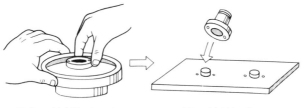

Before: Held by hand               After: Held by jig

**Figure 6-12.  Holding Jig for Glass Holder Pipes**

using both hands symmetrically and using almost no eye motions (see motion economy checkpoints 1, 2, 3, 5, 6, and 11 in Chapter 5).

*Improving the pick-up method for "A" and "B" washers.* The washers had been kept in plastic bags, as shown on the left in Figure 6-11, and the group thought it would be easier to pick them up if they were instead kept in bins such as those shown on the right in Figure 6-11 (see motion economy checkpoint 5 in Chapter 5).

*Adopting a holding jig.* To make two-handed motions possible, they needed to eliminate the holding motion performed by one hand. Realizing this, Asai thought of making a jig that would hold the glass holder pipes in place during the glass assembly process. Figure 6-12 illustrates this problem and its solution. This example is an application of motion economy checkpoint 4 (see Chapter 5).

*Creating continuous operations.* The group decided to use the holding jig throughout the glass assembly process to eliminate manual holding and make possible more two-handed work.

The results of these improvements are listed in the postimprovement therblig analysis chart (Table 6-7) and data chart (Table 6-8). As a result, the improved motions included far less waste and went much more smoothly, as shown in Figure 6-13.

Table 6-9 and Figure 6-14 show that all of the type 2 and type 3 motions (except eye motions) were eliminated, making the operations much more efficient. In fact, the improvement reduced the total number of motions more than 60 percent ($384/624$ = about 61.5 percent).

### Step 11: Trial Run of the Improvement Plan

Encouraged by the improvement results, the group decided to give the new operations a trial run.

### Step 12: Results of Trial Run

The group did not run into any problems during the trial run.

## Table 6-7. Therblig Analysis Chart (After Improvement)

| No. | Work element | Left hand motion | Therbligs Left | Therbligs Eyes | Therbligs Right | Right hand motion | Notes |
|---|---|---|---|---|---|---|---|
| 1 | Set up glass holder pipes | Reach for holder pipes. | ⌣ | | ⌣ | Same as left hand motions. | |
| 2 | | Grasp holder pipes. | ∩ | | ∩ | | |
| 3 | | Carry holder pipes to work table. | ᗐ | ⬯ ⬯ | ᗐ | | Mental work (eye motion) required for aligning and fastening holder pipes onto holding jig. |
| 4 | | Fasten holder pipes onto holding jig. | 9 | | 9 | | |
| 5 | | Let go of holder pipe. | ⌒ | | ⌒ | | |
| 6 | Insert "A" washers | Reach for "A" washers. | ⌣ | | ⌣ | " | |
| 7 | | Grasp "A" washers. | ∩ | | ∩ | | |
| 8 | | Carry "A" washers. | ᗐ | | ᗐ | | |
| 9 | | Align "A" washers with holder pipes. | 9 | | 9 | | |
| 10 | | Insert "A" washers into grooves in holder pipes. | ♯ | | ♯ | | |
| 11 | | Let go of "A" washers. | ⌒ | | ⌒ | | |
| 12 | Insert glass plates | Reach for glass plates. | ⌣ | | ⌣ | " | |
| 13 | | Grasp glass plates. | ∩ | | ∩ | | |
| 14 | | Carry glass plates. | ᗐ | | ᗐ | | |
| 15 | | Align glass plates with holder pipes. | 9 | | 9 | | |
| 16 | | Insert glass plates onto holder pipes. | ♯ | | ♯ | | |
| 17 | | Let go of glass plates. | ⌒ | | ⌒ | | |

## Table 6-7.  Therblig Analysis Chart (After Improvement) (cont'd)

| No. | Work element | Left hand motion | Left | Eyes | Right | Right hand motion | Notes |
|-----|-----|-----|-----|-----|-----|-----|-----|
| | | | **Therbligs** | | | | |
| 18 | Insert "B" washers | Reach for "B" washers. | ∪ | | ∪ | Same as left-hand motions. | |
| 19 | | Grasp "B" washers. | ∩ | | ∩ | | |
| 20 | | Carry "B" washers. | ⌣ | | ⌣ | | |
| 21 | | Align "B" washers with holder pipes. | 9 | | 9 | | |
| 22 | | Insert "B" washers onto holder pipes. | ♯ | | ♯ | | |
| 23 | | Let go of "B" washers. | ⌢ | | ⌢ | | |
| 24 | Fasten nuts | Reach for nuts. | ∪ | | ∪ | Same as left-hand motions. | |
| 25 | | Grasp nuts. | ∩ | | ∩ | | |
| 26 | | Carry nuts. | ⌣ | | ⌣ | | |
| 27 | | Align nuts with holder pipes. | 9 | | 9 | | |
| 28 | | Fasten nuts. | ♯ | | ♯ | | |
| 29 | | Grasp nuts. | ∩ | | ∩ | | |
| 30 | | Carry to box on right. | ⌣ | | ⌣ | | |

Repeat the above three times (to complete eight assemblies)

**Table 6-8. Data Chart (After Improvement)**

| Type | 1 | | | | | | | | | | 2 | | | | | 3 | | | | | Total |
|---|---|---|---|---|---|---|---|---|---|---|---|---|---|---|---|---|---|---|---|---|---|
| Therblig | ∪ | ∩ | ⌣ | 𝟫 | ♯ | ↔ | ∪ | ⌢ | ◯ | No. | ◯ | ◑ | → | ϙ | 𝟾 | No. | ◠ | ⌐ | ↰ | ↳ | No. | |
| Left hand | 20 | 24 | 24 | 20 | 16 | | | 16 | | 120 | | | | | | | | | | | | 120 |
| Right hand | 20 | 24 | 24 | 20 | 16 | | | 16 | | 120 | | | | | | | | | | | | 120 |
| Eyes | | | | | | | | | | | 4 | 4 | | | 8 | | | | | | | 8 |

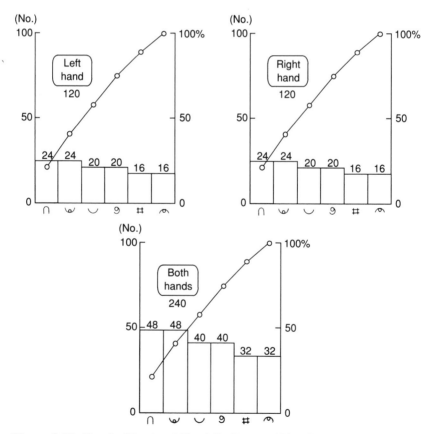

**Figure 6-13. Pareto Charts of Therblig Counts (After Improvement)**

**Table 6-9. Before/After Comparison of Total Motions for Both Hands**

|  | Before Improvement | After Improvement | Difference |
|---|---|---|---|
| Type 1 | 356 | 240 | 116 |
| Type 2 | 16  (15) | —  (8) | 16  (7) |
| Type 3 | 252 | — | 252 |
| Total | 624  (15) | 240  (8) | 384  (7) |

Note: Figures in parentheses are total eye motions.

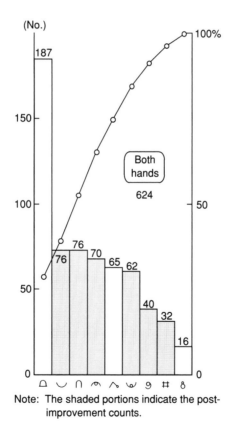

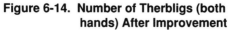

Note: The shaded portions indicate the postimprovement counts.

**Figure 6-14. Number of Therbligs (both
hands) After Improvement**

### Implementing the Improvement Plan

#### Step 13: Implementation and Standardization

The team continues to use the improved method for the glass assembly process and the assembly workers have happily reported that the new method has made their work easier.

Encouraged by his success in leading this improvement project, Asai decided to take on the more challenging task of improving the display mechanism assembly process and began to work on that project.

## CASE STUDY 2: IMPROVEMENT OF STEEL CORD WELDING MACHINE OPERATIONS FOR STEEL RADIAL TIRES

Sadakatsu Tezuka is currently employed at Bridgestone Becalt Steel Cord Company's Tochigi plant, which manufactures the steel cords that are used in Bridgestone's steel radial tires. The Tochigi plant is located in a scenic rural area north of Tokyo.

Tezuka is the immediate supervisor for the steel cord production workshop, which produces the steel cords that form the "backbone" of steel radial tires such as the one shown in Figure 6-15. He enthusiastically participated in the JUSE course in IE for factory managers and is actively involved in QC circle activities.

**Figure 6-15. Steel Radial Tire**

Steel cords are embedded under the tire tread and contribute to improved tire performance (i.e., improved durability, stability, and safety). Cords made of steel offer strength, pressure resistance, and heat resistance that is superior to that offered by belts or cords made of fiber or other materials.

Although rising consumer demand for radial tires has placed pressure on tire companies to speed up their radial tire manufacturing operations, Tezuka noticed that his plant was not operating very efficiently. This prompted him to get together with other managers with a view toward improving his workshop's operations.

## Discovering the Problem

### Step 1: Observing the Workplace

Tezuka first wandered around the workshop simply observing the operations and performing a PQCDSM check. Steel cord bands are the material used in these steel cords. The previous process sends cord bands hanging from holders to Tezuka's workshop. Each finished steel cord is made up of three steel bands that have been welded together (see Figure 6-16). The welding process includes the following elements (see Figure 6-17):

1. Two welded bands are put through a hammer to flatten out any bumps and dents at the weld point and to squeeze the weld point for a more secure bond between the two bands. As shown in part 1 of Figure 6-17, this hammer is applied to the weld points on semifinished products that have already been welded. The hammer is operated with a foot pedal.
2. To check for any remaining unevenness in the weld points, the inspector sets the semifinished steel cord into the B groove of the hammer device and makes sure that it slides smoothly within the groove, as shown in part 2 of Figure 6-17.

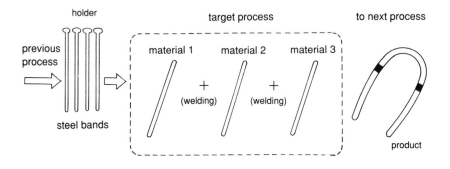

**Figure 6-16. Steel Cord Production Method**

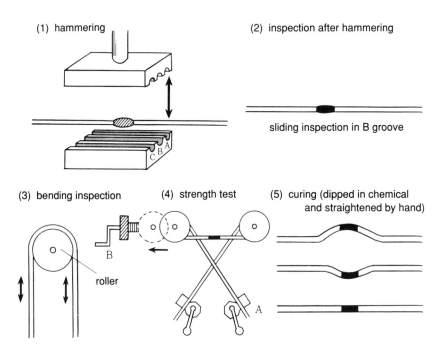

**Figure 6-17. Welding Process**

3. Next, the welded bands are set onto a roller as shown in part 3 of Figure 6-17. They are inspected for flexibility as they are pulled in either direction on the roller.
4. Next, the welded bands are set onto the device shown in part 4 of Figure 6-17, with one end secured at point A, while the other end is stretched by turning the handle at point B. This tests the strength of the weld and the material.
5. Last, the welded bands are dipped in a curing liquid and straightened out by hand.

### Step 2: Identifying Problem Points

The team gathered the results from the PQCDSM check at step 1 and organized them into the chart to begin looking for problem points (see Table 6-10).

## Analyzing Current Conditions

### Step 3: Selecting Problems for Analysis

Tezuka focused his attention on parts of the welding process that his observation showed were possible problems. In this case, he focused on three parts that followed the actual welding: the hammering, testing (bending and strength tests), and curing processes shown in Figure 6-17.

### Step 4: Setting up the Analysis

Tezuka next set up a current-condition analysis.

1. Since the methods to be scrutinized in the analysis included many manual operations, he decided to use therblig analysis.
2. He got out a therblig analysis form and set it up for the analysis by filling in the information requested at the top,

**Table 6-10.  Organization of Problem Data**

| Checkpoint | Yes/No | Description |
|---|---|---|
| Productivity (P): Are there any problems in output volume? | No | Productivity is too low to keep up with the rising demand for steel radial tires. |
| Quality (Q): Are there any quality problems? | Yes | Quality varies due to the lack of standard motions to use in carrying out detailed manual operations. |
| Cost (C): Have costs risen? | Yes | The current operation method is not suffering from rising costs, but improvement in the operation method would not only raise productivity and quality but would also probably lower costs. |
| Delivery (D): Are deliveries late? | No | There are no problems yet, but if demand keeps rising, late deliveries will be inevitable (unless productivity can be improved). |
| Safety (S): Are there any safety problems? | No | No safety problems were discovered. |
| Morale (M): Has worker morale been sinking? | No | No morale problems were discovered. |

such as factory name, operation name, analyst's name, and an operation diagram.

### Step 5: Doing the Analysis

Tezuka then conducted a current-condition analysis. He first carefully observed the hammering process, trying to remain objective about the facts and trying not to see the process only from a supervisor's perspective.

After watching the hammering process several times, he began to distinguish between left-hand and right-hand motions.

He noticed that the operator used his left hand to grasp the bottom of the steel cord and the right hand to remove the steel cord from the holder. He held onto the right end of the steel cord while carrying it to the hammering machine, which he then operated using the foot pedal.

Tezuka also drew a diagram of the hammering operation (Figure 6-18). The hammering can be done in the A or C grooves. Right-handed operators tend to use the A groove and left-handed ones the C groove, although when the more frequently used groove begins showing signs of excessive wear, operators switch to the other one.

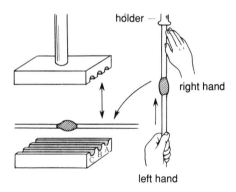

**Figure 6-18. Hammering Operation**

Next, Tezuka closely observed the width inspection process that follows the hammering process. Once a steel cord has been hammered, the operator places the cord into the B groove and holds the cord with both hands while sliding it up and down in the groove. This action deburs the weld site and also indicates if the width is uneven (see Figure 6-19).

After the width inspection, the operator carries the steel cord over to the bending tester for a bending test. As shown in Figure 6-20, the operator sets the steel cord onto the roller and pulls the cord back and forth five times. After observing the strength test several times, Tezuka noted the following sequence of motions:

- After the bending test, the operator sets the steel rod into the strength tester.
- The operator uses his right hand to turn the left and right handles that tighten the cord (see Figure 6-21).
- He uses his left hand to turn the gauge handle and tightens the steel cord to the specified degree to check its strength (see Figure 6-22).
- The operator returns the gauge handle to its original position and then uses both hands to loosen the right and left handles to remove the cord.

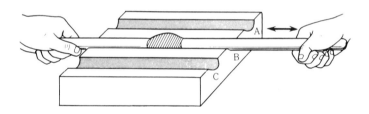

**Figure 6-19. Width Inspection**

Finally, Tezuka observed the operator performing the curing operation. The operator holds the cord that has been taken off the strength tester with both ends of the cord in his right hand. He then dips the weld site into a vat of curing liquid and manually straightens out any bends that have been put into the cord during the tests, as shown in Figure 6-23.

### Step 6: Making the Therblig Analysis Chart

After noting these observations, Tezuka returned to his desk to enter the results onto the therblig analysis form (see Table 6-11). To make later studies easier, he tallied up totals for

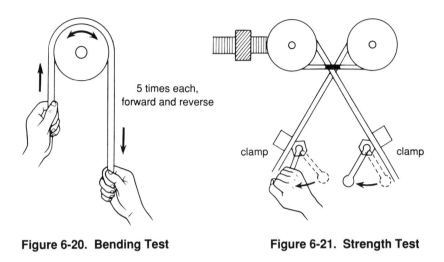

**Figure 6-20. Bending Test**

5 times each,
forward and reverse

**Figure 6-21. Strength Test**

clamp                    clamp

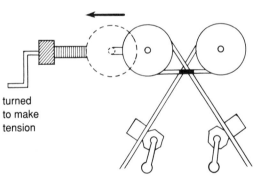

turned
to make
tension

**Figure 6-22. Strength Test**

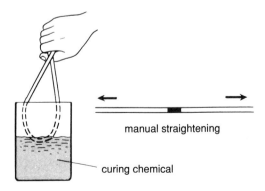

manual straightening

curing chemical

**Figure 6-23. Curing (Manual Straightening)**

### Table 6-11. Therblig Analysis Chart (Before Improvement)

| No. | Work element | Left hand motion | Therbligs Left | Eyes | Right | Right hand motion | Notes |
|-----|--------------|------------------|------|------|-------|-------------------|-------|
| 1 | Hammer-ing | Reach for cord. | ⌣ | | ⌣ | Reach for holder. | |
| 2 | | Grasp cord. | ∩ | | ∩ | Grasp holder. | |
| 3 | | Hold cord. | ⌂ | | ++ | Release cord. | |
| 4 | | " | ⌂ | | ⌣ | Reach for released cord. | |
| 5 | | " | ⌂ | | ∩ | Grasp cord. | Mental action (eye motion) required to set cord into hammering device. |
| 6 | | Carry to hammer. | ⌣ | | ⌣ | Carry to hammer. | |
| 7 | | Position. | 9 | ⊂⊃ | 9 | Position. | |
| 8 | | Use (hammer). | U | | U | Use (hammer). | |
| 9 | Width inspection | Carry to groove B. | ⌣ | | ⌣ | Carry to groove B. | |
| 10 | | Position. | 9 | ⊂⊃ | 9 | Position. | Same as above. |
| 11 | | Transport (slide cord in groove). | ⌣ | | ⌣ | Transport (slide cord in groove). | |
| 12 | | Inspection. | ◊ | | ◊ | Inspection. | |
| 13 | Bending test | Carry to bending tester. | ⌣ | | ⌣ | Carry to bending tester. | |
| 14 | | Set onto roller on tester. | 9 | | 9 | Set onto roller on tester. | |
| 15 | | Hold. | ⌂ | | ⌣ | Pull on cord. | |
| 16 | | Pull on cord. | ⌣ | | ⌂ | Hold. | |
| 17 | | Hold. | ⌂ | | ⌣ | Pull on cord. | |
| 18 | | Pull on cord. | ⌣ | | ⌂ | Hold. | |
| 19 | | Hold. | ⌂ | | ⌣ | Pull on cord. | |
| 20 | | Pull on cord. | ⌣ | | ⌂ | Hold. | |

## Table 6-11. Therblig Analysis Chart (Before Improvement) (cont'd)

| No. | Work element | Left hand motion | Left | Eyes | Right | Right hand motion | Notes |
|---|---|---|---|---|---|---|---|
| 21 | Bending test | Hold. | ⌒(hold) | | ⌒(transport) | Pull on cord. | |
| 22 | | Pull on cord. | ⌒(transport) | | ⌒(hold) | Hold. | |
| 23 | | Hold. | ⌒(hold) | | ⌒(transport) | Pull on cord. | |
| 24 | | Pull on cord. | ⌒(transport) | | ⌒(hold) | Hold. | |
| 25 | | Move to a position where bending is easiest to check. | 8 | | 8 | Move to a position where bending is easiest to check. | |
| 26 | | Check bending. | ◊ | | ◊ | Check bending. | |
| 27 | | Pick up cord. | 9 | | 9 | Pick up cord. | |
| 28 | Strength test | Carry to strength tester. | ⌒(transport) | | ⌒(transport) | Carry to strength tester. | |
| 29 | | Position. | 9 | ⊘ | 9 | Position. | Mental action (eye motion) required to set cord into specified position. |
| 30 | | Insert cord in jig. | ♯ | | ♯ | Insert cord in jig. | |
| 31 | | Release. | ⌒(release) | | ⌒(release) | Release. | |
| 32 | | Stand by. | ⌣(rest) | | ⌣ | Reach for left handle. | |
| 33 | | " | ⌣(rest) | | ∩ | Grasp left handle. | |
| 34 | | " | ⌣(rest) | | ⌒(transport) | Turn handle to tighten cord. | |
| 35 | | Reach for gauge handle. | ⌣ | | ⌒(release) | Release. | |
| 36 | | Grasp. | ∩ | | ⌣(rest) | Stand by. | |
| 37 | | Use (move handle to specified value). | ∪ | | ⌣(rest) | " | |
| 38 | | Return to original position. | 8 | | ⌣(rest) | " | |
| 39 | | Release. | ⌒(release) | | ⌣(rest) | " | |

**Table 6-11. Therblig Analysis Chart (Before Improvement) (cont'd)**

| No. | Work element | Left hand motion | Therbligs | | | Right hand motion | Notes |
|---|---|---|---|---|---|---|---|
| | | | Left | Eyes | Right | | |
| 40 | Strength test | Reach for handle. | ⌣ | | ⌣ | Reach for handle. | |
| 41 | | Grasp. | ⌒ | | ⌒ | Grasp. | |
| 42 | | Loosen handle. | ⌣ | | ⌣ | Loosen handle. | |
| 43 | | Release. | ⌒ | | ⌒ | Release. | |
| 44 | Curing | Reach for cord. | ⌣ | | ⌣ | Reach for cord. | |
| 45 | | Grasp. | ⌒ | | ⌒ | Grasp. | |
| 46 | | Carry cord to right hand. | ⌣ | | 8 | Prepare to receive cord from left hand. | |
| 47 | | Release (cord into right hand). | ⌒ | | ⌒ | Grasp (cord from left hand). | |
| 48 | | Rest. | ⌐ | | ⌣ | Carry cord to curing vat. | |
| 49 | | " | ⌐ | | ⊞ | Dip cord into curing vat. | |

each type of therblig and entered them on data charts and graphs (Tables 6-12 and 6-13).

As you can see from the various motion totals listed in the data chart and graph, there are a lot of type 3 motions (e.g., unavoidable delay [standby] and hold) and also a lot of type 1 motions (transport loaded [carry]). The graph in Table 6-14 organizes these motion totals into work element categories.

Table 6-14 makes it clear that the overwhelming majority of motions are type 1 motions, most of which are carry motions. It also shows that there are a lot of type 3 hold motions. Table 6-14 also shows that the work element containing the largest number of these carry and hold motions is the bending test.

**Table 6-12. Data Chart (Before Improvement)**

| Type | 1 | | | | | | | | | | 2 | | | | | | 3 | | | | | Total |
|---|---|---|---|---|---|---|---|---|---|---|---|---|---|---|---|---|---|---|---|---|---|---|
| Therblig | ⌣ | ∩ | ⌣ | 9 | ♯ | ↔ | U | ⌒ | 0 | No. | ◯ | ◖ | → | ℓ | 8 | No. | △ | ∧ | ⌣ | ⌐ | No. | |
| Left hand | 4 | 4 | 12 | 5 | 1 | | 2 | 4 | 2 | 34 | | | | 2 | 2 | 8 | 3 | 2 | | | 13 | 49 |
| Right hand | 5 | 6 | 13 | 5 | 2 | 1 | 1 | 3 | 2 | 38 | | | | 2 | 2 | 5 | 4 | | | | 9 | 49 |
| Eyes | | | | | | | | | | | 3 | 3 | 3 | | | 9 | | | | | | 9 |

## Finding the Most Important Problems

### Step 7: Identifying the Important Problem Points

Tezuka studied the current-condition analysis results. He found the following problem points to be the most important:

1. There are too many hold and standby (type 3) motions.
2. Even type 1 motions should be trimmed down. In this case, there are too many carry motions, and a way should be found to reduce them.

Having found that 72 of the 98 motions in these operations are type 1 motions, Tezuka decided to concentrate his improvement efforts on that type of motion first. After that, he would take up the problem of the standby motions and other type 3 motions.

## Drafting Improvement Plans

### Step 8: Considering Ways to Eliminate Motions

In these circumstances, it would be difficult to eliminate operations; the welded steel cord had to be deburred and

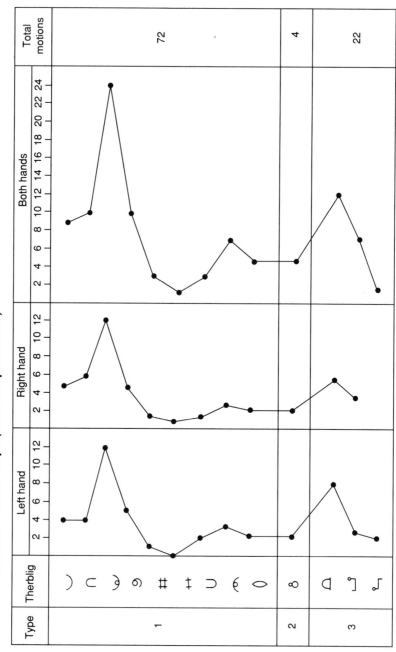

Table 6-13. Hand Movement Graph (Before Improvement)

Table 6-14. Work Element Graph (Before Improvement)

smoothed out, and client specifications made the inspections and tests necessary.

### Step 9: Applying the Other Principles of Improvement — Simplifying, Combining, and Rearranging

While pondering the problems and thinking about the improvement-making principles, Tezuka suddenly realized something: The preponderance of carry motions during the bending test was due to the manual work involved in pulling the cord on the roller and also due to the separation of processes that required the cord to be carried here and there. He then understood that the way to reduce the carry motions was to apply the "combining" principle to integrate the separate processes.

### Step 10: Selecting an Improvement Plan, Predicting the Effects with Therblig Analysis, and Checking the Results

At this point, Tezuka assembled his team of workers, explained the results of the current-condition analysis and the key problems, and then asked everyone to brainstorm ideas for an improvement plan to combine processes.

After a long discussion, the group decided on the following improvement plan. This plan emphasizes checkpoint 7 (the carry motion) from the principles of motion economy (see Chapter 5).

1. *Improvement of bending test and width inspection.*
   - To eliminate the many pull and carry left- and right-hand motion combinations that arise from using just one roller, as shown on the left in Figure 6-24, the group installed two other rollers so that the carry motion would no longer be required. The left picture in Figure 6-24 shows how the bending test can be done using three rollers instead of one.

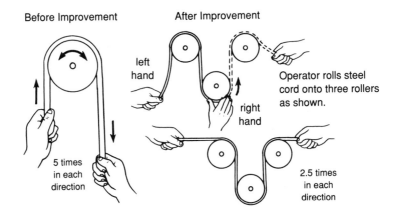

Figure 6-24. **Improvement of Bending Test and Width Inspection**

- The group also came up with a way to combine the bending test with the width inspection by putting width-checking grooves in the three bending rollers (see Figure 6-25).

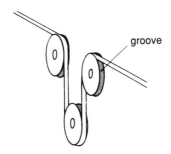

Figure 6-25. **Roller Grooves**

2. *Improvement of cord fastening (during strength test) and curing.* Feeling confident in their plan for combining the width inspection process with the bending test process,

the group turned their attention to the second half of the operations, namely the strength test and curing processes that accounted for 22 of the current total of 49 motions. They were particularly interested in reducing the number of reach-grasp-carry motion sequences.

They considered applying the principle of combination toward this problem, too. As shown in Figure 6-26, the current practice was to first do the strength test, then dip the steel cord into the curing vat and manually straighten out the cord. They came up with the following improvement plan for this problem:

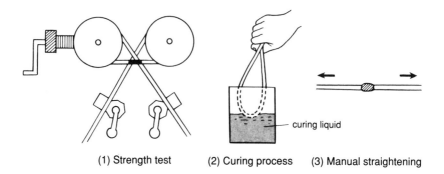

(1) Strength test        (2) Curing process        (3) Manual straightening

**Figure 6-26. Improvement of Strength Test and Curing Process**

- Automate the pulling (strength testing) of the fastened cord. As shown in Figure 6-27, the group designed a tester in which the operator places the cord, then simply pushes a button to activate two cylinders that clamp down on the cord at both ends to hold it in place. Applying checkpoint 4 from the motion economy principles (do not use hands if you can use feet instead), they also designed a foot pedal for pulling the cord to the specified tension point.

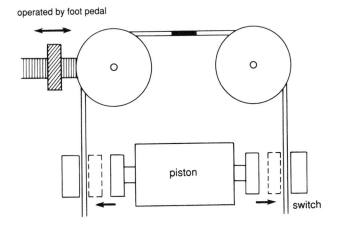

operated by foot pedal

piston

switch

**Figure 6-27.  Automation of Strength Test**

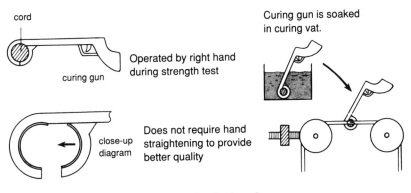

cord

curing gun

Operated by right hand
during strength test

close-up
diagram

Does not require hand
straightening to provide
better quality

Curing gun is soaked
in curing vat.

**Figure 6-28.  Curing Gun**

- To combine the strength test process with the curing
  process, the group devised a "curing gun" that can be
  clamped around the cord during strength testing to
  apply curing liquid to the weld sites (as shown in
  Figure 6-28). The group then filled out a therblig
  analysis chart to get an idea of what effects their
  improvement plan would bring (see Table 6-15).

## Table 6-15. Therblig Analysis Chart (After Improvement)

| No. | Work element | Left hand motion | Therbligs | | | Right hand motion | Notes |
|---|---|---|---|---|---|---|---|
| | | | Left | Eyes | Right | | |
| 1 | Hammer-ing | Reach for cord. | ⌣ | | ⌣ | Reach for holder. | |
| 2 | | Grasp cord. | ∩ | | ∩ | Grasp holder. | |
| 3 | | Hold cord. | ⌂ | | ++ | Release cord. | |
| 4 | | " | ⌂ | | ⌣ | Reach for released cord. | |
| 5 | | " | ⌂ | | ∩ | Grasp cord. | |
| 6 | | Carry to hammer. | ⌣ | | ⌣ | Carry to hammer. | |
| 7 | | Position. | 9 | ⊙ | 9 | Position. | |
| 8 | | Use (hammer). | U | | U | Use (hammer). | |
| 9 | Width inspection and bending test | Carry to width inspection and bending test. | ⌣ | | ⌣ | Carry to width inspection and bending test. | |
| 10 | | Position. | 9 | ⊙ | 9 | Position. | Mental action (eye motion) required to set cord onto three rollers. |
| 11 | | Hold. | ⌂ | | ⌣ | Pull on cord. | |
| 12 | | Pull on cord. | ⌣ | | ⌂ | Hold. | |
| 13 | | Hold. | ⌂ | | ⌣ | Pull on cord. | |
| 14 | | Pull on cord. | ⌣ | | ⌂ | Hold. | |
| 15 | | Hold. | ⌂ | | ⌣ | Pull on cord. | |
| 16 | | " | ⌂ | | ++ | Release cord. | |
| 17 | Strength test and curing | Carry to strength tester. | ⌣ | | ⌣ | Carry to strength tester. | |
| 18 | | Position. | 9 | ⊙ | 9 | Position. | |

**Table 6-15. Therblig Analysis Chart (After Improvement) (cont'd)**

| No. | Work element | Left hand motion | Therbligs | | | Right hand motion | Notes |
|---|---|---|---|---|---|---|---|
| | | | Left | Eyes | Right | | |
| 19 | Strength test and curing | Set into strength tester. | ⧺ | | ⧺ | Set into strength tester. | |
| 20 | | Hold cord. | ⌓ | | ⌒ | Let go of strength tester. | |
| 21 | | " | ⌓ | | ⌣ | Reach for switch. | |
| 22 | | " | ⌓ | | U | Press switch. | |
| 23 | | Release. | ⌒ | | ⌒ | Release. | |
| 24 | | Reach for gauge handle. | ⌣ | | ⌣ | Reach for curing gun. | |
| 25 | | Grasp gauge handle. | ∩ | | ∩ | Grasp curing gun. | |
| 26 | | Use gauge handle. | U | | ⏜ | Carry to cord (weld site) | |
| 27 | | Return to original position. | 8 | | U | Use. | |
| 28 | | Release. | ⌒ | | ⏜ | Carry gun into curing vat. | |
| 29 | | Reach for cord. | ⌣ | | ⌒ | Release. | |
| 30 | | Grasp. | U | | ⌣ | Reach for switch. | |
| 31 | | Hold. | ⌓ | | U | Turn off switch. | |

Tables 6-16 and 6-17 show the significant reduction in carry motions made by these improvements. The work element breakdown of improvement results in Table 6-18 shows how big a reduction in carry motions was made in the width inspection and bending test processes.

**Table 6-16. Data Chart (After Improvement)**

| Type | | | | | | | | | 1 | | | | 2 | | | | | | | 3 | | | | | Total |
|---|---|---|---|---|---|---|---|---|---|---|---|---|---|---|---|---|---|---|---|---|---|---|---|---|---|
| Therblig | ⌣ | ⌒ | ᴗ | 9 | ♯ | ↔ | U | ⌢ | () | No. | ○ | ⊙ | → | ⸯ | 8 | No. | ⌓ | ⌃ | ⌟ | ⌞ | No. | |
| Left hand | 3 | 3 | 5 | 3 | 1 | | 2 | 2 | | 19 | | | | 1 | 1 | 11 | | | | | 11 | 31 |
| Right hand | 5 | 3 | 8 | 3 | 1 | 2 | 4 | 3 | | 29 | | | | | | 2 | | | | | 2 | 31 |
| Eyes | | | | | | | | | | | 3 | 3 | 3 | | | 9 | | | | | | 9 |

As Table 6-17 shows, the improvements brought an increase in use motions. However, this was due to the use of the switches for the automated processes. Table 6-19 tallies up the various type 1, type 2, and type 3 motions before and after improvement. All three types of motion are reduced in all processes except the hammering process, and the overall motion reduction rate is about 40 percent (36/98).

## Implementing the Improvement Plan

### Step 11: Trying Out the Plan

After confirming the effects of the improvement plan, Tezuka gave it a trial implementation.

### Step 12: Checking Results and Implementing the Plan

Having found that the plan brought the expected effects, Tezuka shared the good results with other managers at related operations. The one major drawback of this improvement was that it failed to significantly reduce the hold motions. Realizing this, Tezuka determined to review the operations and attempt further improvements.

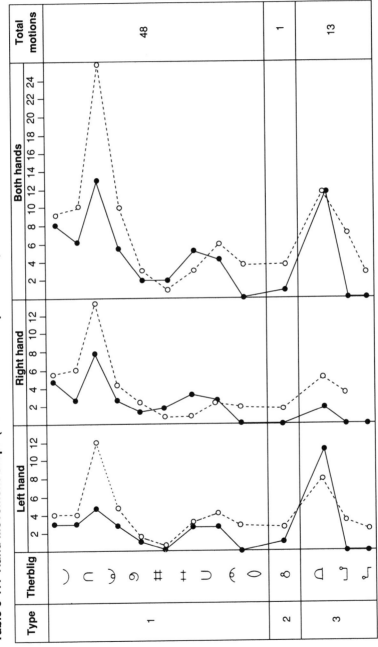

**Table 6-17. Hand Movement Graph (Before and After Improvement)**

Note: The dotted lines show before-improvement totals.

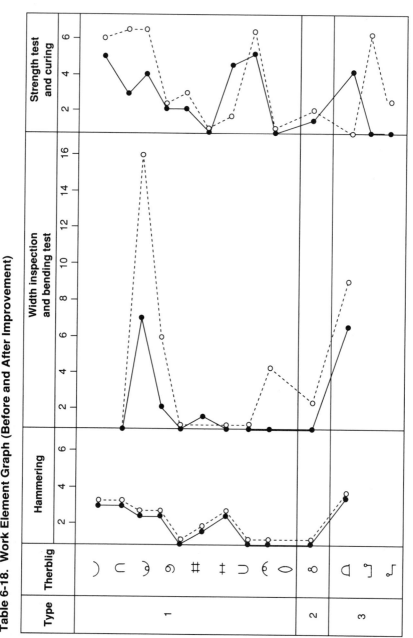

Table 6-18. Work Element Graph (Before and After Improvement)

**Table 6-19. Summary of Motions**

| | Overall Total | | | Hammering | | | Width inspection and bending test | | | Strength test and curing | | |
|---|---|---|---|---|---|---|---|---|---|---|---|---|
| | Before | After | Difference | Before | After | Difference | Before | After | Difference | Before | After | Difference |
| Type 1 | 72 | 48 | 24 | 13 | 13 | — | 26 | 10 | 16 | 33 | 25 | 8 |
| Type 2 | 4 (9) | 1 (9) | 3 | (3) | (3) | — | 2 (3) | — (3) | 2 | 2 (3) | 1 (3) | 1 |
| Type 3 | 22 | 13 | 9 | 3 | 3 | — | 10 | 6 | 4 | 9 | 4 | 5 |
| Total | 98 (9) | 62 (9) | 36 | 16 (3) | 16 (3) | — | 38 (3) | 16 (3) | 22 | 44 (3) | 30 (3) | 14 |

Note: Figures in parentheses indicate eye motions.

# Index

# OTHER BOOKS ON MANUFACTURING IMPROVEMENT

Productivity Press publishes and distributes materials on continuous improvement in productivity, quality, customer service, and the creative involvement of all employees. Many of our products are direct source materials from Japan that have been translated into English for the first time and are available exclusively from Productivity. Supplemental products and services include newsletters, conferences, seminars, in-house training and consulting, audio-visual training programs, and industrial study missions. Call 1-800-274-9911 for our free book catalog.

## Quality Function Deployment
### Integrating Customer Requirements into Product Design
*edited by Yoji Akao*

More and more, companies are using quality function deployment, or QFD, to identify their customers' requirements, translate them into quantified quality characteristics and then build them into their products and services. This casebook introduces the concept of quality deployment as it has been applied in a variety of industries in Japan. The materials include numerous case studies illustrating QFD applications. Written by the creator of QFD, this book provides direct source material on Quality Function Deployment, one of the essential tools for world class manufacturing. It is a design approach based on the idea that quality is determined by the customer. Through methodology and case studies the book offers insight into how Japanese companies identify customer requirements and describes how to translate customer requirements into qualified quality characteristics, and how to build them into products and services.
ISBN 0-915299-41-0 / 400 pages / $ 75.00 / Order code QFD-BK

## Function Analysis
### Systematic Improvement of Quality and Performance
*by Kaneo Akiyama*

As an innovative, flexible company facing new challenges in the 1990s, your organization needs to reexamine continuously the models upon which its operations are based. Function Analysis is a systematic technique for isolating and analyzing various functions in order to better design and improve products. This book gives you a solid understanding of Function Analysis as a tool for system innovation and improvement; it helps you design your products and systems for improved manufacturability and quality. It describes how function analysis is used in the office as well as on the shop floor.
ISBN 0-915299-81-X / 320 pages / $59.95 / order code FA-BK

**Productivity Press, Inc., Dept. BK, P.O. Box 3007, Cambridge, MA 02140 1-800-274-9911**

# The Visual Factory
## Building Participation Through Shared Information
by Michel Greif

If you're aware of the tremendous improvements achieved in productivity and quality as a result of employee involvement, then you'll appreciate the great value of creating a visual factory. This book shows how visual management can be used to make the factory a place where workers and supervisors freely communicate and take improvement action. It details how to develop meeting and communication areas, communicate work standards and instructions, use visual production controls such as kanban, and make goals and progress visible. Over 200 diagrams and photos illustrate the numerous visual techniques discussed.
ISBN 0-915299-67-4 / 256 pages / $49.95 / Order code VFAC-BK

# JIT Factory Revolution
## A Pictorial Guide to Factory Design of the Future
by Hiroyuki Hirano / JIT Management Library

Here is the first-ever encyclopedic picture book of JIT. With 240 pages of photos, cartoons, and diagrams, this unprecedented behind-the-scenes look at actual production and assembly plants shows you exactly how JIT looks and functions. It shows you how to set up each area of a JIT plant and provides hundreds of useful ideas you can implement. If you've made the crucial decision to run production using JIT and want to show your employees what it's all about, this book is a must. The photographs, from Japanese production and assembly plants, provide vivid depictions of what work is like in a JIT environment. And the text, simple and easy to read, makes all the essentials crystal clear.
ISBN 0-915299-44-5 / 227 pages / $49.95 / Order code JITFAC-BK

# JIT Implementation Manual
## The Complete Guide to Just-In-Time Manufacturing
by Hiroyuki Hirano

Here is the most comprehensive and detailed manual we have found anywhere for setting up a complete JIT program. Encyclopedic in scope, and written by a top international consultant, it provides the JIT professional with the answer to virtually any JIT problem. It shows multiple options for handling every stage of implementation and is appropriate to all factory settings, whether in job shop, repetitive, or process manufacturing. Covering JIT concepts, techniques, and tools, and including hundreds of illustrations, charts, diagrams, and JIT management forms, this manual is a truly indispensable tool.
ISBN 0-915299-66-6 / 1000+ pages in 2 volumes / $2500.00 / Order code HIRANO-BK

Productivity Press, Inc., Dept. BK, P.O. Box 3007, Cambridge, MA 02140 1-800-274-9911

# Measuring, Managing, and Maximizing Performance

*by Will Kaydos*

You do not need to be an exceptionally skilled technician or inspirational leader to improve your company's quality and productivity. In non-technical, jargon-free, practical terms this books details the entire process of improving performance, from "why" and "how" the improvement process works to "what" must be done to begin and to sustain continuous improvement of performance. Special emphasis is given to the role that performance measurement plays in identifying problems and opportunities.

ISBN 0-915299-98-4 / 208 pages / $34.95 / Order MMMP-BK

# Performance Measurement for World Class Manufacturing
## A Model for American Companies

*by Brian H. Maskell*

If your company is adopting world class manufacturing techniques, you'll need new methods of performance measurement to control production variables. In practical terms, this book describes the new methods of performance measurement and how they are used in a changing environment. For manufacturing managers as well as cost accountants, it provides a theoretical foundation of these innovative methods supported by extensive practical examples. The book specifically addresses performance measures for delivery, process time, production flexibility, quality, and finance.

0-915299-99-2 / 272 pages / $45.00 / Order code PERFM-BK

# Introduction to TPM
## Total Productive Maintenance

*by Seiichi Nakajima*

Total Productive Maintenance (TPM) combines the American practice of preventive maintenance with the Japanese concepts of total quality control (TQC) and total employee involvement (TEI). The result is an innovative system for equipment maintenance that optimizes effectiveness, eliminates breakdowns, and promotes autonomous operator maintenance through day-to-day activities. This book summarizes the steps involved in TPM and provides case examples from several top Japanese plants.

ISBN 0-915299-23-2 / 149 pages / $39.95 / Order code ITPM-BK

**Productivity Press, Inc., Dept. BK, P.O. Box 3007, Cambridge, MA 02140 1-800-274-9911**

# FACTORY MANAGEMENT NOTEBOOK SERIES
## Case Studies in Improvement
*edited by Esme McTighe*

The Factory Management Notebook Series provides subscribers with several notebooks each year of leading-edge articles and case studies translated and compiled from Japan's NKS Factory Management Journal. The Journal has been reporting on new technology and manufacturing breakthroughs for over 15 years. Its authors are among Japan's most renowned industrial leaders and innovators. The Series' first volume (1991) provides fresh information four times throughout the year (six issues are planned for the 1992 volume) on new developments in a specified subject areas: mixed-model production, visual control systems, autonomation/automation, and Total Productive Maintenance For those who would like a "preview" of the series, the notebooks are also offered individually. Order four-volume set for $600.00.

Mixed-Model Production (Vol.1, No.1) / January 1991 / 184 pages / $175.00 / Order code N1MM-BK

Visual Control Systems (Vol.1, No.2) / April 1991 / 200 pages / $175.00 / Order code N1VCS-BK

Autonomation/Automation (Vol.1, No.3) / Summer 1991 / 200 pages / $175.00 Order code N1AA-BK

Total Productive Maintenance (Vol.1, No.4) / Fall 1991 / 200 pages / $175.00 / Order code N1TPM-BK

# Workplace Management
*by Taiichi Ohno*

An in-depth view of how one of this century's leading industrial thinkers approaches problem solving and continuous improvement. Gleaned from Ohno's forty years of experimentation and innovation at Toyota Motor Co., where he created JIT, this book explains the concepts Ohno considers most important to successful management, with an emphasis on quality.
ISBN 0-915299-19-4 / 165 pages / $34.95 / Order code WPM-BK

**Productivity Press, Inc., Dept. BK, P.O. Box 3007, Cambridge, MA 02140 1-800-274-9911**

# A Study of the Toyota Production System
## From an Industrial Engineering Viewpoint (rev.)
*by Shigeo Shingo*

The "green book" that started it all — the first book in English on JIT, now completely revised and re-translated. Here is Dr. Shingo's classic industrial engineering rationale for the priority of process-based over operational improvements for manufacturing. He explains the basic mechanisms of the Toyota production system in a practical and simple way so that you can apply them in your own plant.
ISBN 0-915299-17-8 / 294 pages / $39.95 / Order code STREV-BK

# Continuous Improvement in Operations
## A Systematic Approach to Waste Reduction
*edited by Alan Robinson*

Now one handy book brings you the world's most advanced thinking on Just-In-Time, *kaizen*, Total Employee Involvement, and Total Productive Maintenance. Here in one volume is a compendium of materials from our best-selling classics by world-famous manufacturing experts. A lengthy introduction integrates the developments of these manufacturing gurus within a twofold theme the elimination of invisible waste and the creation of a work environment that welcomes and institutes employee's ideas. It's a perfect book for your study groups and improvement teams.
ISBN 0-915299-51-8 / 416 pages / $34.95 / Order ROB2C-BK

Productivity Press, Inc., Dept. BK, P.O. Box 3007, Cambridge, MA 02140 1-800-274-9911

# COMPLETE LIST OF TITLES FROM PRODUCTIVITY PRESS

Akao, Yoji (ed.). **Quality Function Deployment: Integrating Customer Requirements into Product Design**
ISBN 0-915299-41-0 / 1990 / 387 pages / $ 75.00 / order code QFD

Akiyama, Kaneo. **Function Analysis: Systematic Improvement of Quality and Performance**
ISBN 0-915299-81-X / 1991 / 288 pages / $59.95 / order code FA

Asaka, Tetsuichi and Kazuo Ozeki (eds.). **Handbook of Quality Tools: The Japanese Approach**
ISBN 0-915299-45-3 / 1990 / 336 pages / $59.95 / order code HQT

Belohlav, James A. **Championship Management: An Action Model for High Performance**
ISBN 0-915299-76-3 / 1990 / 265 pages / $29.95 / order code CHAMPS

Birkholz, Charles and Jim Villella. **The Battle to Stay Competitive: Changing the Traditional Workplace**
ISBN 0-915299-96-8 / 1991 / 110 pages paper / $9.95 /order code BATTLE

Christopher, William F. **Productivity Measurement Handbook**
ISBN 0-915299-05-4 / 1985 / 680 pages / $137.95 / order code PMH

D'Egidio, Franco. **The Service Era: Leadership in a Global Environment**
ISBN 0-915299-68-2 / 1990 / 165 pages / $29.95 / order code SERA

Ford, Henry. **Today and Tomorrow**
ISBN 0-915299-36-4 / 1988 / 286 pages / $24.95 / order code FORD

Fukuda, Ryuji. **CEDAC: A Tool for Continuous Systematic Improvement**
ISBN 0-915299-26-7 / 1990 / 144 pages / $49.95 / order code CEDAC

Fukuda, Ryuji. **Managerial Engineering: Techniques for Improving Quality and Productivity in the Workplace** (rev.)
ISBN 0-915299-09-7 / 1986 / 208 pages / $39.95 / order code ME

Gotoh, Fumio. **Equipment Planning for TPM: Maintenance Prevention Design**
ISBN 0-915299-77-1 / 1991 / 272 pages / $ 75.00 / order code ETPM

Grief, Michel. **The Visual Factory: Building Participation Through Shared Information**
ISBN 0-915299-67-4 / 1991 / 320 pages / $49.95 / order code VFAC

Hatakeyama, Yoshio. **Manager Revolution! A Guide to Survival in Today's Changing Workplace**
ISBN 0-915299-10-0 / 1986 / 208 pages / $24.95 / order code MREV

Hirano, Hiroyuki. **JIT Factory Revolution: A Pictorial Guide to Factory Design of the Future**
ISBN 0-915299-44-5 / 1989 / 227 pages / $49.95 / order code JITFAC

Hirano, Hiroyuki. **JIT Implementation Manual: The Complete Guide to Just-In-Time Manufacturing**
ISBN 0-915299-66-6 / 1990 / 1006 pages / $2500.00 / order code HIRANO

Horovitz, Jacques. **Winning Ways: Achieving Zero-Defect Service**
ISBN 0-915299-78-X / 1990 / 165 pages / $24.95 / order code WWAYS

Ishiwata, Junichi. **IE for the Shop Floor 1: Productivity through Process Analysis**
ISBN 0-915299-82-8 / 1991 / 208 pages / $39.95 / order code SHOPF1

Productivity Press, Inc., Dept. BK, P.O. Box 3007, Cambridge, MA 02140 1-800-274-9911

Japan Human Relations Association (ed.). **The Idea Book: Improvement Through TEI (Total Employee Involvement)**
ISBN 0-915299-22-4 / 1988 / 232 pages / $49.95 / order code IDEA

Japan Human Relations Association (ed.). **The Service Industry Idea Book: Employee Involvement in Retail and Office Improvement**
ISBN 0-915299-65-8 / 1990 / 294 pages / $49.95 / order code SIDEA

Japan Management Association (ed.). **Kanban and Just-In-Time at Toyota: Management Begins at the Workplace** (rev.), Translated by David J. Lu
ISBN 0-915299-48-8 / 1989 / 224 pages / $36.50 / order code KAN

Japan Management Association and Constance E. Dyer. **The Canon Production System: Creative Involvement of the Total Workforce**
ISBN 0-915299-06-2 / 1987 / 251 pages / $36.95 / order code CAN

Jones, Karen (ed.). **The Best of TEI: Current Perspectives on Total Employee Involvement**
ISBN 0-915299-63-1 / 1989 / 502 pages / $175.00 / order code TEI

JUSE. **TQC Solutions: The 14-Step Process**
ISBN 0-915299-79-8 / 1991 / 416 pages / 2 volumes / $120.00 / order code TQCS

Kanatsu, Takashi. **TQC for Accounting: A New Role in Companywide Improvement**
ISBN 0-915299-73-9 / 1991 / 244 pages / $45.00 / order code TQCA

Karatsu, Hajime. **Tough Words For American Industry**
ISBN 0-915299-25-9 / 1988 / 178 pages / $24.95 / order code TOUGH

Karatsu, Hajime. **TQC Wisdom of Japan: Managing for Total Quality Control**, Translated by David J. Lu
ISBN 0-915299-18-6 / 1988 / 136 pages / $34.95 / order code WISD

Kato, Kenichiro. **I.E. for the Shop Floor 2: Productivity through Motion Study**
ISBN 1-56327-000-5 / 1991 / 224 pages / $39.95 / order code SHOPF2

Kaydos, Will. **Measuring, Managing, and Maximizing Performance**
ISBN 0-915299- 98-4 / 1991 / 208 pages / $34.95 / order code MMMP

Kobayashi, Iwao. **20 Keys to Workplace Improvement**
ISBN 0-915299-61-5 / 1990 / 264 pages / $34.95 / order code 20KEYS

Lu, David J. **Inside Corporate Japan: The Art of Fumble-Free Management**
ISBN 0-915299-16-X / 1987 / 278 pages / $24.95 / order code ICJ

Maskell, Brian H. **Performance Measurement for World Class Manufacturing: A Model for American Companies**
ISBN 0-915299-99-2 / 1991 / 448 pages / 45.00 / order code PERFM

Merli, Giorgio. **Total Manufacturing Management: Production Organization for the 1990s**
ISBN 0-915299-58-5 / 1990 / 224 pages / $39.95 / order code TMM

Mizuno, Shigeru (ed.). **Management for Quality Improvement: The 7 New QC Tools**
ISBN 0-915299-29-1 / 1988 / 324 pages / $59.95 / order code 7QC

Monden, Yasuhiro and Michiharu Sakurai (eds.). **Japanese Management Accounting: A World Class Approach to Profit Management**
ISBN 0-915299-50-X / 1990 / 568 pages / $59.95 / order code JMACT

Nachi-Fujikoshi (ed.). **Training for TPM: A Manufacturing Success Story**
ISBN 0-915299-34-8 / 1990 / 272 pages / $59.95 / order code CTPM

**Productivity Press, Inc., Dept. BK, P.O. Box 3007, Cambridge, MA 02140  1-800-274-9911**

Nakajima, Seiichi. **Introduction to TPM: Total Productive Maintenance**
ISBN 0-915299-23-2 / 1988 / 149 pages / $39.95 / order code ITPM

Nakajima, Seiichi. **TPM Development Program: Implementing Total Productive Maintenance**
ISBN 0-915299-37-2 / 1989 / 428 pages / $85.00 / order code DTPM

Nikkan Kogyo Shimbun, Ltd./Factory Magazine (ed.). **Poka-yoke: Improving Product Quality by Preventing Defects**
ISBN 0-915299-31-3 / 1989 / 288 pages / $59.95 / order code IPOKA

NKS/Esme McTighe (ed.). **Factory Management Notebook Series: Mixed Model Production**
ISBN 0-915299-97-6 / 1991 / 184 / $175.00 / order code N1-MM

NKS/Esme McTighe (ed.). **Factory Management Notebook Series: Visual Control Systems: Visual Control Systems**
ISBN 0-915299-54-2 / 1991 / 194 pages / $175.00 / order code N1-VCS

NKS/Esme McTighe (ed.). **Factory Management Notebook Series: Mixed Model Production**
ISBN 0-0-56327-002-1 / 1991 / 200 pages / $175.00 / order code N1-AA

Ohno, Taiichi. **Toyota Production System: Beyond Large-scale Production**
ISBN 0-915299-14-3 / 1988 / 162 pages / $39.95 / order code OTPS

Ohno, Taiichi. **Workplace Management**
ISBN 0-915299-19-4 / 1988 / 165 pages / $34.95 / order code WPM

Ohno, Taiichi and Setsuo Mito. **Just-In-Time for Today and Tomorrow**
ISBN 0-915299-20-8 / 1988 / 208 pages / $34.95 / order code OMJIT

Perigord, Michel. **Achieving Total Quality Management: A Program for Action**
ISBN 0-915299-60-7 / 1991 / 384 pages / $45.00 / order code ACHTQM

Psarouthakis, John. **Better Makes Us Best**
ISBN 0-915299-56-9 / 1989 / 112 pages / $16.95 / order code BMUB

Robinson, Alan. **Continuous Improvement in Operations: A Systematic Approach to Waste Reduction**
ISBN 0-915299-51-8 / 1991 / 416 pages / $34.95 / order code ROB2-C

Robson, Ross (ed.). T**he Quality and Productivity Equation: American Corporate Strategies for the 1990s**
ISBN 0-915299-71-2 / 1990 / 558 pages / $29.95 / order code QPE

Shetty, Y.K and Vernon M. Buehler (eds.). **Competing Through Productivity and Quality**
ISBN 0-915299-43-7 / 1989 / 576 pages / $39.95 / order code COMP

Shingo, Shigeo. **Non-Stock Production: The Shingo System for Continuous Improvement**
ISBN 0-915299-30-5 / 1988 / 480 pages / $75.00 / order code NON

Shingo, Shigeo. **A Revolution In Manufacturing: The SMED System**, Translated by Andrew P. Dillon
ISBN 0-915299-03-8 / 1985 / 383 pages / $70.00 / order code SMED

Shingo, Shigeo. **The Sayings of Shigeo Shingo: Key Strategies for Plant Improvement**, Translated by Andrew P. Dillon
ISBN 0-915299-15-1 / 1987 / 208 pages / $39.95 / order code SAY

**Productivity Press, Inc., Dept. BK, P.O. Box 3007, Cambridge, MA 02140  1-800-274-9911**

Shingo, Shigeo. **A Study of the Toyota Production System from an Industrial Engineering Viewpoint** (rev.)
ISBN 0-915299-17-8 / 1989 / 293 pages / $39.95 / order code STREV

Shingo, Shigeo. **Zero Quality Control: Source Inspection and the Poka-yoke System**, Translated by Andrew P. Dillon
ISBN 0-915299-07-0 / 1986 / 328 pages / $70.00 / order code ZQC

Shinohara, Isao (ed.). **New Production System: JIT Crossing Industry Boundaries**
ISBN 0-915299-21-6 / 1988 / 224 pages / $34.95 / order code NPS

Sugiyama, Tomo. **The Improvement Book: Creating the Problem-Free Workplace**
ISBN 0-915299-47-X / 1989 / 236 pages / $49.95 / order code IB

Suzue, Toshio and Akira Kohdate. **Variety Reduction Program (VRP): A Production Strategy for Product Diversification**
ISBN 0-915299-32-1 / 1990 / 164 pages / $59.95 / order code VRP

Tateisi, Kazuma. **The Eternal Venture Spirit: An Executive's Practical Philosophy**
ISBN 0-915299-55-0 / 1989 / 208 pages/ $19.95 / order code EVS

Yasuda, Yuzo. **40 Years, 20 Million Ideas: The Toyota Suggestion System**
ISBN 0-915299-74-7 / 1991 / 210 pages / $39.95 / order code 4020
**Audio-Visual Programs**

Japan Management Association. **Total Productive Maintenance: Maximizing Productivity and Quality**
ISBN 0-915299-46-1 / 167 slides / 1989 / $749.00 / order code STPM
ISBN 0-915299-49-6 / 2 videos / 1989 / $749.00 / order code VTPM

Shingo, Shigeo. **The SMED System**, Translated by Andrew P. Dillon
ISBN 0-915299-11-9 / 181 slides / 1986 / $749.00 / order code S5
ISBN 0-915299-27-5 / 2 videos / 1987 / $749.00 / order code V5

Shingo, Shigeo. **The Poka-yoke System**, Translated by Andrew P. Dillon
ISBN 0-915299-13-5 / 235 slides / 1987 / $749.00 / order code S6
ISBN 0-915299-28-3 / 2 videos / 1987 / $749.00 / order code V6

Returns of AV programs willl be accepted for incorrect or damaged shipments only.

**TO ORDER:** Write, phone, or fax Productivity Press, Dept. BK, P.O. Box 3007, Cambridge, MA 02140, phone 1-800-274-9911, fax 617-864-6286. Send check or charge to your credit card (American Express, Visa, MasterCard accepted).

**U.S. ORDERS:** Add $5 shipping for first book, $2 each additional for UPS surface delivery. CT residents add 8% and MA residents 5% sales tax. For each AV program that you order, add $5 for programs with 1 or 2 tapes, and $12 for programs with 3 or more tapes.

**INTERNATIONAL ORDERS:** Write, phone, or fax for quote and indicate shipping method desired. Pre-payment in U.S. dollars must accompany your order (checks must be drawn on U.S. banks). When quote is returned with payment, your order will be shipped promptly by the method requested.

**NOTE:** Prices subject to change without notice.